12.12.12

REINVENTED
LIFE

DAMION S. LUPO
&
CHRISTOFER C. ASHBY

Kiny,
Here it my soul bare
to share w/ the world.
Hope it inspires
you toward great
reinvention Joe,

Much love,
Damion

Reinvented Life
Copyright © 2012 by Damion S. Lupo and Christofer C. Ashby

Inquiries should be addressed to:
Reinvented Life
12407 MoPac Expwy. N.
#250-405
Austin, Texas 78758

www.ReinventedLife.com

First Edition

First Printing December 12, 2012

Edited by: Rick Lewis
Cover Design: Rebecca Bretz
Layout Design: Jake Muelle

ISBN print: 978-0-9764754-6-0
ISBN electronic: 978-0-9764754-7-7

1. Self-Help 2. Psychology 3. Business 4. Spiritual

Printed in the United States of America

Sections: PSYCHOLOGY / SELF HELP / BUSINESS

TABLE OF CONTENTS

Foreword 9

Introduction 11

Chapter 1: Our Reinvented Life Stories 15

Damion's Story 15
    My Vision 16
    Before & After 17
    Post-Trigger Event .19
    The Gift 20
Christofer's Story 22
    A Process and Its Consequences 23
    The Synergy of Reinvention 24
    Industrial Age 25

Chapter 2: Trigger Event 27

Theory 28
Damion's Story 29
    My Own Personal Alamo 29
Christofer's Story 33
    A Case of Mistaken Priorities 33
    A Chance Meeting and a New Direction 35
    Log of Lessons Learned 38
Questions & Actions 39

Chapter 3: Consciousness. 41

Theory 42
    Self. 42
    Thinking Time. 44
Damion's Story. 45
    Guidance 45
    Keeping Your Own Power 46
    Power to Reinvent 47
    Responsibility—Get Some! 48
    You & Your Credit Report 48
    Relationships—Confessions of a Serial Dater 49
    Everything Starts in the Mind 51
    Keeping the False Self Safe 52
Questions & Actions 54

Chapter 4: Higher Order Consequences 57

Theory 58
    First, Second and Third Order Consequences 58
    Relationships 59
    Retail Therapy 60
    Food 61
    Root—Instant Gratification. 64
    Six Human Needs. 64
Damion's Story. 75
    Money 75
    Love 77
    Health. 79
Questions & Actions 81

Chapter 5: Success vs. Fulfillment .85

Theory 86
    Mediocrity 88
Damion's Story. 90
    Ferrari 550 90
    Higher Education Tokens. 93
    True Purpose 94
    The Parable of the Honeybee. 96
Questions & Actions 97

Chapter 6: Stillness. 99

Theory 100
Damion's Story. 101
    Yoga 101
    Fear vs. Faith. 103
    Severing Old Connections .103
    Consistency 106
    Full Potential 107
    The Meltdown 109
    Stillness in Love 111
    Throwaway Society. 111
Questions & Actions 112

Chapter 7: The Runway. 115

Theory 116
    ...But First, a Slight Digression
        into Aviation Metaphors. 116
    Understanding and Designing
        Your Reinvention Runway 117

The Convenient Change of Plan 119
Inexcusable Excuses 120
Our Runways 122
Christofer's Story 122
Options and the Black Swan Event 124
Lessons Learned. 126
Damion's Story. 127
Questions & Actions 128

Chapter 8: Metrics 131

An Overview 132
Christofer's Story 133
An Awakening In Paris 135
The Process Begins—Research. 136
Lessons Learned. 138
Summary 139
Questions & Actions 140

Chapter 9: Action-Correction Cycle 145

Theory 146
Education System—Class Idiot Billionaire 148
Law of Awareness. 148
Pain. 149
Accountability Partners 152
Damion's Story. 153
Money 153
Tracking 154
Visceral Spending. 155
Wellness 156
Relationships 158

Course Correction 159
Two Minds 159
Cycles 161
Money 161
Career 162
Relationships 162
Health 163
Questions & Actions 164

Chapter 10: Bucky 5: Osmotic Adaption 167

Theory 168
Blind Spots 169
Damion's Story 170
Thinking Types 171
Can I vs. Should I 172
Instinctual Vetting 172
Proximity 174
Process 175
Christofer's Story 177
A Sudden Change of Perception 179
Summary 181
My Current Inner Circle List 181
Questions & Actions 183

Chapter 11: Simplicity 185

Christofer's Story 186
Shelter from the Storm of Acquisition 187
Damion's Story 188
Questions & Actions 189

Epilogue 193

FOREWORD

We all have a part to play in the evolution of Consciousness. Most simply, that part would be the sharing of our life experiences and our trying to communicate what we have learned from them. Doing this creates a process of co-evolution, a process that alloys us to evolve together. That is what Damion and Christofer are attempting to do in their writing this book. They are trying to share what they have learned on their journeys, often dug out of the ashes of their mistakes. But, the mistakes are not the issue. What they learned and want to share is. Their willingness to share the full range of their thoughts and experiences, mistakes as well as triumphs, is what make this book so valuable.

The heart of the message of this book is the notion of "Reinvention." This simple term, in and of itself, teases us into the process. Think about it: the "Re" in "Reinvention" infers the idea that something is occurring for a second time. What is occurring again is "Invention." In the context of this book, what is being Reinvented is one's "self," our "self," ourselves, our idea of who we think we are.

Reinvention of self would be meaningless without an understanding of what "self" is and without examining the experiences that result from what we believe our "self" to be. Therefore, "Reinvention" is about raising awareness about the *self that we believe we are,* and exposing it as being merely an "Invention"—and thus, something that can be Reinvented.

Damion and Christofer are here to help wake us up to the fact that we can "Invent" a new self, to explain to us how they themselves achieved Reinvention, to discuss the setbacks and traps they encountered along the way, and—above all—to help us follow in their footsteps of Reinvention.

Most of us are not aware that the "self" that we experience as our "self" was invented. It is literally made up. We live as if who we are is something completely static and stable, as if that "who" is something over which we have very little say or control. We tell ourselves that, "We are just born the way that we are," without any awareness that there is actually no definitive "me" at the center. As a result, we fail to recognize that our experiences are the direct result of our living our lives in the mind of an artificial, invented "me." It's as if we live in a fog of misunderstanding that leads to a life that is unconscious and unfulfilling.

This book is a gift. It's your opportunity to learn from someone else's mistakes. Use Damion and Christofer's experiences and insights to see more deeply into how life works. Learn about the connection between one's idea of oneself and the kind of life that that self leads to. Share with them in the lessons that they learned, and explore with them the ideas that they offer about "Reinventing" yourself. Allow their sharing to inspire you and assist you in moving out of your fog.

Enjoy!

—Dr. Frank Allen

INTRODUCTION

The environment is changing, the world is shifting, and modern life is evolving at an exhilarating rate. Many of the systems we rely on to maintain our way of life (lifetime employment, job security, a comfortable retirement) are undergoing massive change. Though not always a resource we use in our daily life, our inherent creative abilities as human beings to adapt, survive and thrive represent an enormous untapped resource. To adapt you must be massively flexible. To reinvent any part of your life, you must be willing and able to make conscious change and critical assessments based on the truth.

Though this book contains many stories, the heart of it lies in the individual authors' reinvention of their respective lives, the process of finding their paths to reinvention, and the actual tactical process of their reinvention.

This book is not a self-help course, nor does it provide any shortcuts to becoming wealthy or healthy. It is the story of two ordinary people who—out of necessity, ambition and extraordinary tenacity—were able to reinvent their personal and professional lives. The details of their experiences, plus a few provocative questions and actions, will possibly provide the insight, framework and impetus to consider reinventing aspects of your own life.

Why bother reinventing? We reinvent when we must. When elements of your life become intolerable, your own subconscious can direct you towards a single, unbearable moment—your "trigger event." This is the inception of a transitional opportunity to create a new form and focus for the relevant part or parts of your life.

This transitional opportunity (as defined by Ilya Prigogine) is called Perturbation. This event is triggered by the absorption of energy into a body (you) until it vibrates to a point where it must either break down into basic units and reform at a higher level/frequency, or fall back to its previous level by escaping the energy inflow.

Your trigger event is a form of perturbation where you've taken on enough energy (positive or negative) to the point when you will either break apart and reform at a new higher level, or will fall back to the status quo. The trigger event is where you can no longer take in and take on the same energetic input and stay in the same form. It's the moment when the necessity of change is the only option.

The trigger event is your opportunity and gateway to a Reinvented You. The trigger event has an acutely binary outcome: you either walk through the door or you don't. Most people will, for a host of reasons, choose to stay in the current state of their life rather than venture into the unknown. It's an understandable dilemma, as the process of intelligently reinventing your life or career requires critical thinking, tools and processes beyond the random and undirected manner in which most people lead and live (either consciously or unconsciously) their lives.

There is a well-published school of thought that the ideal life and treasures we desire (or think we deserve) are simply a product of "thinking positive" and "attracting what you visualize." Although there are reported cases (primarily found in the New Age section of your favorite bookstore and *The National Enquirer*) of lady luck making an unannounced appearance and the "dreamer/visualizer's" wishes being made manifest, this is not a recommended strategy or a replacement for the real work that must be done to change your current circumstances. If lady luck does exist, she is highly fickle, usually choosing to bestow her gifts on those who have little apparent need for her.

The truth is far simpler and less random. Once you've committed to going down this road and acknowledging the intolerable areas of your current life, retreating to your former circumstances ceases to be alternative. The clearer you get and the more progress you make, the more you will be tested. Things and people will pull on you to come back, to surrender to the way of the black crabs and tall poppies, but it's up to you to fight through and incrementally emerge into your Reinvented Life.

Here's to your reinvention and the courage to take the Red Pill.

RED PILL

def.

We are all at a crossroads. One road is the same one we've travelled all of our lives. The other leads to the rabbit hole where the real world awaits. A reference to *The Matrix*, to take the Red Pill is to choose to explore the truth, a path that leads only forward and never in reverse. Alternatively, you can take the Blue Pill and choose to stay unconscious and enjoy the tasty pseudo-steak. The choice is yours. What color do you choose?

1

OUR REINVENTED LIFE STORIES

DAMION'S STORY

Just five years ago, a mega-size consumption addiction was the driving force in my life, fueled by a desperate need to spend a million a year on my American Express Black card. I was hell bent on consuming and lying my way into success. My only vision for my life was buying, owning and controlling more. The truth is I was a deeply lost human being.

That's all my life had been for more than a decade. I was about as far from conscious as one could be. I spent time, energy and resources buying for the sake of buying, earning more to spend more, acting the part of a hyper little consumer.

I consumed as much as I could—food, toys, relationships, anything—in a futile attempt to satisfy my need to feel like a success, to have tokens of proof I could display as if each one was a badge of accomplishment. I believed consuming three pounds of king crab legs and a bottle of wine at every meal, zipping around in a Titanium Ferrari, jet setting around the world in first class, owning a monster portfolio of a hundred rental houses, and being the king of my own 5,000-square-foot castle on the golf course was proof positive that I'd succeeded and was happy.

MY VISION

From the very beginning I had goals and ambitions. I had goals about having goals. I focused on producing and on achieving. I thought I'd found the secret of success, that whatever I wrote down would spring to life. In large part that's true. It's also true that if you have a giant list of material goals, your life will largely be a material life because that's what you'll focus on and that's what you'll put your energy into manifesting—for better or worse.

My singular vision was to "get more." I sought more houses, more money, more power, more glory. One would think I was attempting a second coming of Alexander the Great given my salivating desire for the holy grail of success. Year after year I added more assets to my portfolio, conquered more women, owned more of the world, and it was never enough.

The truth about having a big goal strategy focused on things and stuff is that it's an unsustainable cycle that never ends and spirals towards misery. But, boy, did I buy into it hook, line and sinker. I bought into it and I lived it. I spun around on the merry-go-round until I'd consumed every ounce of air and flew off, unconscious and blue.

A deeper look using my mind's eye of today reveals a very different story. What I see now, in truth, is an ever-indulging little boy, dwelling on shiny toys in a vain attempt to prove his self-worth. All the while, I was actually destroying my net worth with ever more debt and an unsustainable lifestyle based on fear and manipulation. The mind of my former self was so twisted in the lies I told myself, the black-and-white truth was beaten mercilessly into a murky gray until the gray became intolerable.

BEFORE & AFTER

Back then, I had what I thought was a world-class strategy for changing my viewpoint and mindset. I moved a dozen times in less than a decade, each time looking for the perfect location to be happy. I learned new cutting-edge techniques for doing bigger deals and making more money. I hired a ridiculously expensive mentor who charged me $3,000 for thirty-minute calls. I dated all sorts of interesting and amazing women from all different backgrounds. I tried the rich approach with millions in the bank and five empty bedrooms in my castle. I tried the broke approach with nothing in the bank, living out of my car or an occasional hotel. I tried all sorts of different ways of thinking and doing. Ultimately I found myself in the same place every single time. I found myself back in my own mind.

Then, in 2009, at the worst of the real estate crash and the great recession, my unconscious brought together the necessary elements for me to finally wake up. I experienced my trigger event (see Chapter 2), which busted up my routine patterns of unconscious behavior like a hard stomp on the accelerator breaks through the gummed-up crap in a car engine. It blows out the crusty gunk, freeing the engine to perform. So it was with me. One powerful "boom" event gave my mind a chance to transform and reinvent.

When my trigger event happened and my reinvention really began, my being seemed to separate from me, taking on an energy of its own. At times I watched, not helpless to act, but not clear on how to control it. And for the first time, I was at peace with the lack of control.

Looking back on it now, this peace reminds me of the time I jumped out of a plane and my parachute failed. It was a tandem jump, meaning I was attached to my instructor. The moment he told me to tuck under him so he could cut loose the failing parachute, I remember having a peace come over me in a flush of calm and a total release of control. There was absolutely nothing I could do to affect my life or death at that moment, and it was probably the most peaceful second or two of my entire life.

I felt no fear, no pain, no regret, only silence and absolute freedom. I didn't see the proverbial light, but I certainly found myself engulfed in something far more powerful than my feeble attempts to control everything. I was free and at peace, and I had zero control of anything. And then the instructor cut us free of the primary chute and released the reserve chute, just in time to save our lives.

POST-TRIGGER EVENT

After my big bang event in 2009, my life and mind were thrown into a blender.

I was even more directionless than before. I tried to distract myself with all sorts of external stimuli from women to cars, alcohol to adventure. The problem with all these things was that they did nothing towards helping me find the truth. They were simply masking the pain of acknowledging the operating system I'd been running and the carnage I'd been leaving in my wake.

The idea of acknowledging and owning my mind scared the hell out of me so I stayed distracted with engaging experiences, all the while pretending to be happy with self-medicating types of activities that released endorphins and numbed the pain of being me. I was definitely doing the "old fake it 'til you make it" routine.

Later I learned the secret is that it's not about a mindset *change* but a mind *exchange*. Many people I encounter believe they can change their lives by simply thinking or doing something differently. This is false. I used to think the very same thing.

THE GIFT

The gift I received from my work with Dr. Frank Allen was the truth that all of the changes, adjustments and improvements I was making were within the same mind I'd always had, and therein was the problem. The mind that had changed perspectives was still the mind that was causing the problems.

During the second year of work on tearing out my guts and dissecting my mind, I tripped into the realization that I had to exchange my mind, not change my mind. The old mind didn't go away because I had a new thought or new way to do something. Even when I started operating from my new mind, the old mind still tried to participate alongside my new mind of truth on a regular basis. The *action-correction cycle* allowed me to strengthen the new mind until it ran the show and the old mind was more of a buzzing fly. Sure, it was annoying and never seemed to go away, but it couldn't alter the mind in charge or the truth that it acquired.

Over the following two years, I spent a majority of my time finding consciousness, digging into the highest level consequences I could see, and exploring the difference between success and fulfillment.

Physically, my journey took me from coast to coast. Mentally, it took me deep inside my soul, to a place I'd never been. I ventured to a place where acknowledging the truth of my past brought tears and anger that I could have ever been such a man. The tears and the anger continued the trigger event and radically broke the spell of addiction, the addiction drama, control and chaos.

During these years I went deep inside, asking questions I'd never asked. I found solace in moments of silence and the study of yoga and Aikido. Everything changed because my mind was exchanged. I simplified virtually everything in my life and let go of the drama and the need for excess material things that had driven my satisfaction in my old life.

One of the greatest benefits of the mind exchange and reinvention has been the friendships and level of connection I have with the people in my life. My friends are all different today because I am different. Those who have not evolved and moved into truth are not reflective of me today, nor do they interest me—no matter how much they may have interested the man I was a few years ago.

The shift, the change, the reinvention is truly one-way and there's no going back. My mind smiles and laughs a little at the thought of going back because the idea that my former self with my previous mind could ever be me again makes about as much sense as me being a golden retriever. The shift is permanent, and the gratitude is eternal.

CHRISTOFER'S STORY

1988: It's the final concert of my thirteen-city solo tour of The People's Republic of China, and I'm backstage getting ready to play my first encore, The Miller's Dance by Manuel de Falla. In the past three weeks I have performed fifteen concerts, taught four master classes, cut a record, performed live in front of more than 100,000 people, visited beautiful and fascinating cities, and—most importantly to me at the time—was recognized and acknowledged by my peers and audiences as a virtuoso.

I had dedicated a large part of my life to becoming a great musician and performer, and by all appearances, the years of hard work and sacrifice are paying off. The only problem with this situation is that I have absolutely no passion for what I am doing, am deeply unhappy, creatively and emotionally dead, and feel like I'm living in a bad dream.

Life is elsewhere, I think, *but I am still here.*

1992: It's 11:00 p.m., and I have not slept for two days. Ernst and Young, the firm with whom I am employed, is engaged to assist the European Bank for Reconstruction and Development (EBRD) with its due diligence on a $90 million credit facility for a recently privatized power generation company. Two of my colleagues and I are asked (once again) to present and discuss our audit of three off-take agreements between the power company and its fuel providers. The bank's underwriters and risk management people ask for a recess and two hours later return with a term sheet. The facility is approved.

Rather than join my colleagues for a celebratory drink, I decide to walk back to my hotel and stop in front of St. Paul's Cathedral. Looking at the magnificent portico of the cathedral, I am suddenly reminded of a time in the not-too-distant past when I stood in this same location waiting for a cab to take me to a rehearsal for my one of my London recitals. I am completely overwhelmed with gratitude and thanks for having been able to totally reinvent my career as a classical musician to work in corporate finance.

A PROCESS AND ITS CONSEQUENCES

If, before walking onto the stage for my final performance in Beijing, someone would have told me that in three years I would be in London, discussing a due diligence report with a room full of bankers, I would have been skeptical though not unhappy with the idea. If the same person would have told me that I would be back in Beijing performing the same repertoire in the same hall, I would have been deeply unhappy.

Before discussing the "how," it is more important to summarize the "why" of such an enormous reinvention of my life and career. The core reasons were:

1. Although still very excited about music, I had completely lost the passion for performing, was totally bored with the repertoire, and had become completely fed up with the lifestyle and inherent limitations of the discipline;
2. I wanted to have a level of financial freedom and wealth that as a classical guitarist would never happen;
3. I wanted specific material things;
4. I wanted a life with more financial security;
5. I wanted to be like my heroes, who were not musicians but investment bankers.

So how did this massive change unfold, and what was the first step towards its realization? What sort of person did I have to become, and what did I have to leave behind to reinvent my career and life? What really drove me to make this change, and was reinvention a product of luck, hard work or grace?

THE SYNERGY OF REINVENTION

Reinvention is not one-dimensional. It's an interlocking tapestry of actions and events between the various pieces of one's life. If your health is bad and receives no attention, your financial life will suffer. If your finances are a mess and you are chronically stressed about paying your bills, it will affect your health. If your love life is lacking or disengaged and your solution is to seek excitement or connection by frequenting strip clubs, taking drugs or drinking, your finances will suffer.

Sharing our stories is something we are compelled to do, and our only motivation in doing so is to assist others in their ongoing or planned reinventions. We also realized the power and strength in knowing when something is appropriate to share and also when the power is in the silence. Both can be every bit as powerful as the other.

INDUSTRIAL AGE

At some point we have to divorce ourselves from everything that seemed right in the industrial age. Working hard equals guaranteed success; thirty-year jobs with one organization; eating meat and potatoes is smart; men work, women don't; religion equals spirituality; war is inevitable; etc. We literally have to swap our mind for another if we wish to reinvent. A slight shift results in an off-balanced version of the same you, a wobbly former self with a different eyeglasses prescription. We need new eyeballs, not new lenses.

When we insist on honesty and integrity in our lives, the people, events and circumstances that do not personify truth gradually disappear and are replaced by people, events and circumstances that reflect our newly found belief system. The forms outside of us that we see are reflective of the level of truth inside us.

This is the story of our reinventions, the experiences and lessons learned.

2
TRIGGER EVENT

def.

An event or situation, which provides an opportunity for transformational change or reinvention

> *Trigger moments are created to test the readiness of the mind or to course correct into the physical truth of the mind. The choice you have in those moments is to shift horizontally in status quo or to go vertical, as if being launched by a cannon. The explosion is the same, but the trajectory is within you.*
>
> —Dyokido

THEORY

A trigger event usually happens by our own creation. It's a moment when the dam breaks and unleashes a torrent of information awareness and clarity about something you have to do (or something you can no longer do) in this life. This something becomes the dominant thought in your mind. Things start to crumble, and emotion is high. The intensity and suddenness of this initial insight either launches you into action or induces a mental paralysis. This, according to Ilya Prigogene's Theory of Dissipative Structure, is called Perturbation.

The reason the event is of your own creation is because your mind has summoned the necessary conditions for your reinvention. The need to change becomes a drive in order for your environment to be in harmony with your mind. Without a shift you'll be in conflict and constantly out of alignment. The reborn mind that's emerged as your new mental operating system creates an environment for the trigger event to surface.

In life we have rhythms and habits. These are often unconscious and stay the same for years, leading to both positive and negative results. When the negative results compound to a point that the damage is too deep, the usual outcome is to run into a self-imposed brick wall that knocks us down and turns our physical or mental world upside down. At some point the gnawing gets so strong we don't have the choice of staying in our current state (or staying the same person with the same mind). The event could be a moment in time when you suddenly break down in tears or you wake up in a cold sweat knowing something is drastically wrong. When you know something is wrong but lack the mental vocabulary to articulate it, the prospect of burying it is a nonstarter.

DAMION'S STORY

MY OWN PERSONAL ALAMO

Crack...crack...crack...The echoes of knuckles rapping on my maple wood front door could be heard from across the little Spanish casita in Arizona where I'd been holed up for the last half year. On edge and leery of opening the door to an unknown stranger, I approached with concern and unease. Could the stranger be a process server with a lawsuit? Could it be a pissed off ex-girlfriend who tracked me down, wanting to punch me in the face for breaking her heart? Maybe it was a Girl Scout selling Thin Mints? Yeah right, maybe it was the Easter Bunny. My mind raced...

I didn't know, and in a heightened state of fear my mind created the worst.

It was winter 2008, and for the previous six months I'd been going through the motions, projecting a guy people would like—a charismatic success story, a self-made millionaire who built wealth from dust and was happy and content. But deep down I felt extreme anxiety, knowing something was deeply wrong. I was on edge constantly, watching over my shoulder and keeping the shadows within view. I was suspicious of everyone and everything, from the slightest noise at night to any certified piece of junk mail without a return address in my mailbox.

A few years earlier I'd gone through a week of hell at the Mayo Clinic, being poked and prodded by a team of doctors, all struggling to figure out what was wrong with me. Something was wrong, but we were all looking in the wrong place, my body. My body had seemed close to death, showing indications of failure after passing out while taking a leak one night in San Diego.

My Mayo trip had taken place just a few weeks after keeling over with stabbing pains in my guts, certain I was dying, lying face down on a cold concrete bathroom floor in Costa Rica. The problem wasn't my body, but my body was the external reflection and projection of the problems in my mind and soul, where the true source of my pain lay hidden. The doctors never could find anything in my blood or on X-ray.

But now, the knock at the door told me everything I needed to know. My reaction sealed the deal and created a trigger point that started a chain reaction of events that resulted in my Reinvented Life.

In nervous trepidation I inched up to the door and peered through the peephole until I could see FOUR bodies outside with badges on their chests and guns on their hips. HOLY F@%KING CRAP!

I froze momentarily and then realized I had to hide. I needed to escape, but what if they—whoever they were—had the house surrounded. Okay, new plan. The best idea would be to quietly tiptoe back to the guest room and hide in the closet. This is where I'd be safe. Fortunately, I'd put cardboard on the side windows next to the front door so the badged men couldn't see me slipping away into the darkness (something I was skilled at from years of training).

I went to the closet and waited. I waited for what seemed an eternity until I figured it was safe to venture out, hoping they'd given up. Still in fear and panic, I decided to hop out the window and climb over the fence, hoping to sneak around the neighborhood to where I could spy on my front door and anyone waiting there for me.

I made my way through prickly pear cacti, amid the ugly pig-like javelinas, who snorted their annoyance. I eventually made my way to the street in front of my house, saw the vacant path and front door. I peered in all directions for anyone looming in the bushes, waiting to attack, arrest or accost me for any ol' reason. Nobody.

So I ran up to the front door and found a brown envelope with the letters IRS on it. Oh, crap.

All the blood drained out of my face as I opened the envelope and pulled the papers out. *Now what?* I thought. What else could possibly go wrong? I'd already lost my house, the woman I wanted to marry, most of my fortune, my success, my Ferrari… everything. Was this the trigger that would push me into utter bankruptcy or even into death?

"Dear Ms. Dorman," it read.

Holy crap, this letter wasn't even for me! Those men with guns weren't looking for me! They wanted the previous occupant!

This was my trigger event—a moment in time that would lead me down a course away from the fear that consumed me, from the anxiety that left me on paralyzed a bathroom floor in Central America, from the pain that sent me to the Mayo Clinic, certain I was terminal, living on borrowed time.

Fear had evolved into a stress that blew up my life in every way imaginable. I then began a journey through the fear, from unconscious actions into conscious being.

Two years later, the man in the mirror was bright and clear, a reflection of peace. I was hardly recognizable as the frightened little man hiding from himself in a closet in the dusty desert town of Alamo, Arizona. That rap, rap, rap at the front door triggered a one-way shift into permanent reinvention.

CHRISTOFER'S STORY

A CASE OF MISTAKEN PRIORITIES

The primary reason I enjoyed performing recitals and concerts was that it provided me with the opportunity to travel the world. The repertoire and general dynamics of performing had become less and less enjoyable over time, and the music to which I was increasingly attracted was more ethnic in nature (Blues, Flamenco, Balinese Gamelan, Classical Chinese) and not in the genre in which I was able to make a living.

Around this time, I started to work as both a session player and arranger on numerous recording projects that had nothing to do with classical music. It was quite exciting to be able to work in television (composing and performing), movies and the occasional rock album. As interesting and financially lucrative as these new opportunities were, they restricted my ability to travel, and it soon became clear that something had to change as the life I was living was not terribly fulfilling.

I decided to put my energy into applying for a university teaching position and started the process of sending out resumes and interviewing. The strategy was to teach during the scholastic year and then use my summer vacation to travel and play music. I was offered a teaching position at a Midwestern university, and it seemed that everything was going according to my plan. The life I thought I wanted was starting to materialize. But during the drive to the airport for my return trip to California, I had an ominous feeling that new plan was not going to work out as planned.

Arriving back at my home five days after the interview and job offer, I found the following four letters in my mailbox:

1. An employment contract from the university;
2. An invitation from the cultural attaché of the People's Republic of China inviting me for a twelve city tour of the country;
3. A recording contract from the China Record Company;
4. And a letter announcing that I had been granted a postdoctoral Fulbright Fellowship to study Flamenco music in Spain.

After about three seconds of soul searching, I called the university and told them I was not taking the job, accepted the Fulbright Fellowship, and confirmed the China tour.

Ten weeks later, I was in Tokyo, Japan, giving a master class before commencing the China tour. In spite of my previous decision to cease performing, this sudden change of fortune appeared to be some sort of cosmic gift (or joke). Moving to Spain, an international tour of China and a recording contract, though still not addressing my concerns of financial security, seemed to be good options.

A CHANCE MEETING AND A NEW DIRECTION

While sitting in the Narita, Japan, airport with luggage, I struck up a conversation with a complete stranger who, seeing my touring case, asked if I was in a band. A rather talkative person, he informed me that he was a manager in Mellon Bank's private equity group, had been a music major in college, and had switched his degree to business so he could make a good living and not live hand to mouth as a musician. After about thirty minutes of relatively pleasant conversation, he asked if he could be blunt. Assuming he was going to ask about my love life or recent master class in Tokyo, I agreed to the proposed interrogation. The questions and answers were as follows:

"Do you make any money doing this?"

I tried to come up with a few defensive answers to show I was successful and doing well financially, although my deceptive strategy did not work. I decided to level with my new friend and tell him about my financial concerns.

"How much are you making on this tour?"

I knew that my airfare and travel expenses were covered, although I was not sure who was going to pay me and how much. After all, I rationalized, it is a great experience and will eventually lead to something "very lucrative."

"What is the upcoming lucrative thing that this will lead to?"

Doing my best to salvage any remaining vestige of self-esteem, I attempted to come up with some creative ideas about more tours, recording contracts, etc., but in the end I had no clue how to answer the question.

"So you flew halfway around the world, are going to play a dozen concerts, make a record and give master classes, all without knowing how much or if you will be paid? Are the promoters charging admission and who will receive the royalties from the record?"

Since I was cornered in a conversation that I had been attempting to have with myself for the last six months, all I could do was answer that I did not know.

"How much savings do you have?"

Easy enough, I was proud to say that I had $45,000 in Security Pacific Bank.

"That is great," he said. *"But you will never have any financial success unless you start asking some hard questions and stop deluding yourself that there is some big payoff in this profession. Maybe there is golden ring, although I advise you to do some research and get the facts."*

In the world of arts, it's generally accepted that no one speaks about money, and there's an unspoken fear (perhaps for good reason) that any discussion of money will coarsen or degrade one's talents. His seemingly innocuous questions really shook me up, and I started to think about all of the things I was and had been doing with my "profession"—things that weren't really generating any income at the time, nor was that likely to change.

At this point in the conversation/interrogation, after having been completely eviscerated by my new friend/advisor/executioner, the only things about which I was absolutely certain were:

1. I was about to commence a tour of China and didn't even know if I was going to be paid for my performances;
2. I was going to make a record, but I hadn't discussed what or how I was going to be paid;
3. My travel and accommodations were paid;
4. I was upset and somewhat embarrassed.

He spent the next three hours talking about the costs of various things (houses in Connecticut, boats, custom tailored suits, more boats, etc.) and how much income one needed to generate to afford such items. I'd never considered the ownership of anything other than my instruments and now was aware of the cost of owning an apartment in New York City, a Ferrari Testarossa and a first class ticket on JAL (New York to Japan), amongst other things. Rather than be discouraged, I decided to undertake my first due diligence project of finding out the real financial metrics of my chosen profession and, perhaps being somewhat naïve, also decided that it was time to pursue the getting of money.

The experiences that led to my reinvention from a classical musician to having a career in corporate finance began with a simple question from a complete stranger with whom I never had any further contact. Although (post university interview) I had felt that something was terribly wrong, I decided to not give any attention to my intuition. I made myself believe that a Fulbright Fellowship, China tour and record contract were a "sign" that my many concerns were a nothing more than a sign of weakness. I tried to suppress (with a little help from the universe) a number of difficult questions by attempting to return to my comfort zone, and it did not work. Instead, I had been forced to face up to those very hard questions about my career from an unexpected source in an unimagined location.

LOG OF LESSONS LEARNED

1. Sometimes, if a really great question is asked, the universe will provide an equally great answer, although you might not always hear the answer in the usual places.
2. If you are not interested in money, then it won't really matter what you do as you probably won't have any of it come your way. If you are interested in it, figure out very quickly:

    a. How much you need to have the things that you want
    b. If your chosen profession can provide what you need
    c. If someone else in your chosen profession has achieved what you want and how they did it

3. Great creativity and resourcefulness is not exclusively the domain of musicians, painters, sculptors, etc. If you want to be great at what you do, first find out if you can be great and then either develop a system of constant improvement or borrow someone else's.

4. Once you decide to start down the path of a reinvention, make sure you're clear on the reason you're doing it and then make some plans for the outcome of your actions. Allow yourself to be insanely inquisitive, willing to ask the hard (and sometimes idiotic) questions, and ready to receive brutally honest answers from people whose opinions are relevant and matter. Absolutely never make any assumptions about any aspect of such a critical endeavor as reinventing your life/career.

5. Be cognoscente and delineate between inner and outer work on your new path. It is very easy to confuse the two and develop a practice of non-action or too much action.

6. Even though we would all like to "follow our bliss," it is very possible that your bliss could bankrupt you.

QUESTIONS & ACTIONS

1. What moment have you had recently that froze you, pissed you off, made you scream, or felt like you were absolutely lost and something was wrong?

2. What did this moment say to you in your gut?

3. Who do you know and trust that you can share this experience with for perspective?

3
CONSCIOUSNESS

def.

1. The state of being awake and aware of one's surroundings.
2. The awareness or perception of something by a person.

*Projection makes Perception. The world you see is
what you gave it, nothing more than that. But though
it is no more than that, it is not less. Therefore, to you
it is important. It is the witness to your state of mind,
the outside picture of an inward condition. As a man
thinketh, so does he perceive. Therefore, seek not to change
the world, but choose to change your mind about the
world. Perception is a result and not a cause.*

—From "A Course in Miracles"

THEORY

Consciousness is about waking up to your truth.
Consciousness isn't about moral or ethical distinctions, *i.e.*,
good versus bad or right versus wrong. Consciousness is about
awakening to a higher level of enlightenment where you're able
to answer the questions:

1. What is?
2. What is not?
3. What is true?

SELF

The key is to be honest with yourself. A wonderful way of
knowing if you're in a state of truth is by the amount of anxiety
that comes with your answer after asking something of yourself.
Oftentimes the stress and anxious feelings are associated with
"knowing something is wrong/untrue."

When we ask, "What is true?" and then acknowledge the truth, the anxiety subsides. The moment we take the truth and act in opposition to it, we feel the pain of conflict and the break in integrity. Our truth and our motion are not in sync, and thus we are not at peace.

Being conscious is being comfortable with saying what needs to be said and simultaneously being comfortable not saying anything at all. It's not about forcing your truth upon the world; it's about seeing it and having light shine on it from deep introspection. Once you've considered what "it" is and how it's impacting you, you can decide what (if anything) to do with it. The opposite of this (which is the normal state of interaction for most people) is being in conversation without intention, with a need to be heard instead of contributing anything of value.

The idea and belief that you're doing someone a favor by telling them the truth is false and not at all useful to a conscious person. This need to get something off your chest (and the smug sense of satisfaction you feel when doing so) is simply a service to your ego.

You'll know you're going into a higher state of consciousness by the growing number of questions you ask and the amount of distinctions you can make. The better you get, the finer the distinctions you'll be able to make.

THINKING TIME

Blocking out a specific period of time to think and journal your thoughts is an invaluable tool to develop and shift your consciousness. Start with a question, write it down, and then let the mind go. Whatever shows up in the flow gets shot out onto the paper or screen. Nothing is judged; it's just an open flow, a channel into the mind.

The power to get clarity through placing a question in front of you and chronicling your spontaneous thought process is truly breathtaking. It's far more common practice to make a hasty "gut" reaction decision in the heat of the moment as opposed to allowing our minds to work on a specific question or problem. Writing out the big question at hand and asking, "What is true within this question?" is an extremely powerful structure for developing conscious thought.

DAMION'S STORY

GUIDANCE

My continuing journey of shifting into deeper consciousness (from a general state of unconsciousness) happened through hundreds of hours of study with a mentor/counselor who acted as a guide into truth. I didn't go kicking and screaming like a lot of people in therapy. I went because I knew there were things I just couldn't see myself without getting help.

The smartest decision I've ever made was seeking the guidance of a world-class expert on the subject of truth, which in turn has given me an extraordinary understanding of and relationship with my own path and truth.

Ask yourself, who helps me see my truth?

Therapy or having a coach can be an amazing tool for shifting into consciousness. Alternatively, these activities can serve as an ego-driven hour of "getting things off your chest." The delineation between the two is about intention, the "why" behind the action. When I go into a room with my therapist, I arrive without an agenda other than seeking deeper truth. I go in and ask, "What is the truth about the present?"

Ask yourself, what is the truth about my present?

This might seem like a strange question, but you'll get the hang of it quickly. Whatever answer shows up, just keep asking, "What else is true?" Create a list, and you'll start to get clarity.

One doesn't necessarily have to visit a therapist to dive deeper into consciousness. However, the focus on truth in that hour and space you share with someone who has real domain expertise is undeniably a more valuable experience than 1,000 hours of random chat with a friend or family member.

Every week I walk into the office and ask the question, "What is true?" I've been doing this for almost two straight years. Why? No, I'm not crazy (although some might argue this point). It's because every week I get the chance to remove one more layer of falsehoods so that my soul is more transparent and I'm ever more clear and conscious.

KEEPING YOUR OWN POWER

Ever had someone say something behind your back or heard a rumor that made you mad? With the internet and the ability to run the rumor mill anonymously, developing a reputation or ruining a reputation can happen in a heartbeat.

Before my reinvention I was highly sensitive to what was written about me on blogs and even the reviews on Amazon pertaining to my first book. I created meaning for myself around the opinions of others, and I gave my power away, the power of truth.

Deep down the shift into consciousness brought the truth to the surface. I realized that bits and pieces of what was being written about me were true and the reason I was mad was because I was embarrassed about them. I fought to disavow the stuff online, but the reason it really bothered me was because I was deeply ashamed of who it revealed me to be.

The shift into indifference was the shift into consciousness. At last, my truth matched my actions. When those two things merged into alignment, my concern over anyone else's opinion vaporized. Today, if someone says I'm a fathead jerk or a womanizing liar, the words no longer matter because I'm clear about who I am and no longer afraid of being exposed for something, for anything. The past stuff no longer represents my present self and the truth of who I am.

In 2007 and 2008, I didn't want anyone to know who I was. When anything was written about me online, I defended it or denied it. The partial truth in the stuff that was published hurt me, and I hated what it said about me and about who I was.

Before reinvention I was afraid of what others might say because I was afraid the ugly stuff might just be true. When you yourself don't know what's true, how can you believe yourself when you say others are wrong? I was lost and didn't bother to ask, "What is true?" I just looked for social validation and feedback that felt good. I lived and died by the opinions of others, mostly strangers. Seems slightly insane to me today.

POWER TO REINVENT

The power to reinvent and go conscious was always in me as it is in you. It was in my trigger event that I realized I had to do something totally different, and part of that was to ask radically different but simple questions.

Today, I'm almost totally neutral about what others say. Someone once said, "It's none of my business what you think about me." Every once in a while, someone will Google me either out of curiosity—a fact that used to scare me to death because there were so many pieces of ugly truths out there that I appeared to be some sort of monster.

RESPONSIBILITY–GET SOME!

Now when someone looks me up on the internet, I don't worry about what they read because these days at worst I'm the cookie monster, not the fire-breathing dragon I was in years past. I'm very clear about who I am today and totally at peace with it.

I fully acknowledge my past, my mistakes and my idiot choices. I take responsibility, knowing full well I hosed a bunch of stuff. In terms of mistakes, I'm pretty sure I've made several lifetimes' worth already. The only way mistakes equate to being a failure is when we don't learn from them. That's the only failure. Failing at something is a learning process, even when it creates an enormous mess.

YOU & YOUR CREDIT REPORT

These days, it seems we are defined by a combination of our credit report and the result of the first page on a Google search. Credit scores tell a story about past decisions, though a number has no bearing on defining the actual worth of a person. Can Google's algorithm and search results determine the truth behind someone and rank their life's activities and artifacts correctly? Part of my reinvention was to become clear on how I reacted to both of these things.

When I lost several of my properties to foreclosure, it felt horrible and I saw myself as a failure. I had my self-worth tied to my net worth, and I saw a loser in the mirror. My credit score went from 792 to 440 in a matter of months. Maybe you've had this happen; certainly you know people who have. The stigma of a bad credit score can be painful and debilitating so long as it becomes the benchmark by which we define ourselves. I had done just that, and my pathetic credit score was a representation of my choices and values before my reinvention.

The choices and values that led to a 440 score are no longer a part of my psyche and have nothing to do with my being or how I've operated for the last couple of years. They simply represent the choices of my previous mind.

Whatever you do—never, ever let your credit report define you. It's simply a number, and your reinvention partly depends on *you not* defining yourself by that number. Consciousness is finding the truth, not letting a credit agency tell you what you are.

RELATIONSHIPS-CONFESSIONS OF A SERIAL DATER

One of the warning signs that I was a bona fide serial dater was when the host of VH1's "The Pickup Artist" suggested to me that I was more than qualified to have a reality show about online dating given the sheer number of dates I had originated from internet dating sites. I would have been a great spokesperson for the site if it was about dating quantity vs. quality in the process of finding a suitable partner.

With woman after woman, I kept asking, "What's wrong with them?" I would never ask what was wrong with me. The answer to that would have been brutal so I just pointed the finger at the women I was with until the never-ending questions about them simply exhausted me and I gave up.

During my reinvention, one of my questions to myself was: "Why am I alone, and why do I keep blowing up these relationships?" I finally realized I was starting off in a lie and was adapting myself to them and to the path of the lie until it was such a jumbled mess that I had to run away to avoid facing the cleanup.

The problem is that it's not possible to fix a lie. And since I was the one lying, I was the problem. That realization kind of sucked, but it was true. And the truth can be fixed, while the lie can't be.

Today I show up as me, fully present and honest. I don't show up as a lie. I don't build a façade or try to woo anyone with an image of something that isn't me. I'm a big fan of courting, but I won't do or be anything that isn't authentic. I consistently and routinely share myself with others in a deeply connected way, something I didn't do in the past.

Here are some questions to ask yourself:

- *What parts of your relationship could you be more authentic with? Any part of a relationship that is based on anything other than the truth will mess up everything else because it will eat at you.*
- *What are you tolerating that you shouldn't?*
- *What do you need to take responsibility for?*

EVERYTHING STARTS IN THE MIND

The most important part of consciousness is that moment when we realize everything is in our mind: the truth, the lies, the reality, the perspective, everything. Once we come to this realization, we can start to have control and can affect and create change instantly.

If you believe yourself to be powerless about an election and your job will eventually be affected by cheap foreign labor (or the value of the Yen against the dollar, or anything else over which we have no control and is outside of us), you are 100% correct. We are powerless because we've handed away the responsibility for determining what's true to an outside power. Alternatively, we have the choice to decide that the election and/or the Yen has no impact on us and direct our thoughts and efforts towards what is true.

"But wait!" you say, "The outcome of this election and the new healthcare laws, the rampant defense spending, the increase in taxes, the unbalanced budget, etc., will all have an impact on me!" But I ask, do they? What is true? How do they have an impact on you unless you let them?

Alternatively, how much control do you have as soon as you ask, "What is true?" My contention is you have all the power and all the control as soon as you enter truth.

KEEPING THE FALSE SELF SAFE

Coping and security comes in many forms. Coping with fear can be dealt with temporarily in all sorts of ways. Making a lot of money to protect one from being homeless. Marrying a high-power, high-earning person. Joining a gang. Building walls or moats around your house. There are endless possibilities.

In my case I lived in a panicky state of fear with endless sleepless nights, and my safeguard against the boogeyman was guns.

At the height of my fear, I had a personal arsenal that would have made a small army envious. I remember telling myself I was a "collector." I remember reading some article about how they were a great investment and pretending I was investing in them. The truth was, I used them to give me a false sense of security. Think about the things you create in your mind to provide the illusion of security. Do they actually make you safe?

I was literally at war, protecting the lies in my mind, fighting off the truth. The guns represented my armament and defenses to protect me from the ever-possible invading army of truth. I'd convinced myself on some level that the more guns I had the safer I was.

The logistics of actually utilizing my private arsenal were inconceivable—though the more I stocked up, the safer I thought I'd be. At least that was the feeling I got for a second or two when I bought another gun or visited my in-home armory.

When the truth surfaced and I realized the deeper reason behind all the guns, I gasped at the insanity of what I had created and had a fire sale, liquidating the ridiculous arsenal in a month. The arsenal contradicted everything that mattered to me when I acknowledged what it was and why it was part of my life. It contradicted all that I was and embodied, my faith in something greater than and outside of fear. Getting rid of all the Bang! Bang! metal allowed me to open up and be free of what the guns represented.

What are your "guns" that you have to protect you from the things you fear?

The guns were a symbol of unconsciousness, of living in fear. They were a lie—and lies can't be fixed, only abandoned. Once

I acknowledged the truth, the guns ceased to be relevant. Remember, a mistake is only a failure if you don't learn from it. The first step in learning from a mistake is acknowledging it. Once a mistake is acknowledged, the power fades and course correction can begin.

QUESTIONS & ACTIONS

1. Open up your journal. (Go buy one if you don't have one.) Write three things you have or do in your life that you think makes you happy? For each of these things, right now, write the reasons that they make you happy. Just ask, "How does this make me happy?"

2. What is the one big question that you have been mulling over in your mind that, were it resolved, would allow you to live a more fulfilling life? Take time right now and write three possible solutions for it.

3. What is one thing you're lying to yourself about? To figure this out, think about what makes you uncomfortable, anxious, stressed or nauseous. Ask the question, "What about this is a lie, what might be a lie, what part of the lie do I like?"

4. What do you use to protect you? Guns, tall fences, opulence in consumption, money, lies?

4
HIGHER ORDER CONSEQUENCES

Def.

A result or effect of an action or condition.

> *Believe nothing because a wise man said it.*
> *Believe nothing because it is generally held.*
> *Believe nothing because it is written.*
> *Believe nothing because it is said to be divine.*
> *Believe nothing because someone else believes it.*
> *But believe only what you yourself know to be true.*
> —The Buddha

THEORY

Generally, consequences are things that happen as a result of our actions. We may choose to describe them in other ways (reaping what we have sown, karmic reactions, emotional bank accounts), but in the natural world all causes have effects. Nothing happens in a vacuum; all thoughts and actions have consequences. If we are perceptive, we begin to learn which actions and thoughts (causes) bring us things (effects) that we desire and which bring us unwanted outcomes.

FIRST, SECOND AND THIRD ORDER CONSEQUENCES

First Order consequences are the immediate results and feelings, both pleasure and pain, from an action or choice we make.

Second Order consequences are the longer-term results and ramifications (pleasure or pain) that come about through action or choices. These future consequences can often be known at the time of the initial decision, although rarely by one who is acting in an unconscious manner.

Third Order consequences relate to the fundamental needs of every human being. These are the universal motivators that drive all human action.

The key to finding peace is to seek alignment between the three and eliminate conflict(s) between them in the actions and choices you make. If conflict exists, the priority should be to satisfy the Second and Third Order consequences at the expense of the First Order. Ironically, most problems in our lives are the result of satisfying the First at the expense of the Second with the illusion of temporarily satisfying the Third.

RELATIONSHIPS

CONFLICT BETWEEN FIRST AND SECOND ORDER CONSEQUENCES

Someone is in a committed relationship and decides to have an affair. In having the affair, the feelings, excitement, stimulation, bliss and intrigue of engaging in the affair satisfy the First Order desire of immediate gratification. The Second Order consequence of this action is the jeopardizing of the adulterer's pre-existing long-term, committed relationship. Once the initial excitement/satisfaction dissipates, the process of "managing" the real-world effect(s) on the marriage (destroying trust with a partner, compromising of goals, contracting an STD) usually expedite the manifestation of the Second Order consequence (a relationship in jeopardy).

RETAIL THERAPY

CONFLICT BETWEEN FIRST AND SECOND ORDER CONSEQUENCES

Shopping for the acquisition of nonessential items, unlike infidelity, is a universally accepted practice in which the First Order consequence of immediate gratification is morally and socially embraced. It's difficult (unless you live a monastic life) to escape the constant barrage of marketing where one is incessantly badgered into feeling that only the purchase of the newest gizmo from Apple, the latest fashionable threads from Lululemon, and/or a shiny new car (to replace our shiny slightly-less-new car) will make you achieve a state of bliss and contentment.

The thrill of buying and pride of owning brings an immediate rush of pleasure, not unlike the famous Coney Island act where Mille the chicken receives a pellet of corn after dancing to "God Bless America." (Sadly, this act is a recent casualty of Hurricane

Sandy.) Due to an impeccable combination of internal/external brainwashing and rationalization, both the avian actor and the shopper are fulfilling their need for pleasure by pursuing an entirely random and unrelated action insisted upon by the people watching them,

The Second Order consequences of unfettered "retail therapy" usually shows up on the next billing cycle of the shopper's credit card statement. Any delayed sticker shock can be quickly rationalized with the placebo of a minimum payment and the hope of yet another voyage to the mall.

FOOD

CONFLICT BETWEEN FIRST AND SECOND ORDER CONSEQUENCES

The quick purchase and rapid consumption of fast food is one of the most efficient delivery systems of First Order consequences.

The Second Order consequences of its consumption (body fat, sluggishness, sickness) are initially mitigated by the availability of infomercial-acquired exercise regimes, drugs (sprinkle a little Xenical or Phentermine on your next waffle bowl), and TV shows in which morbidly obese First Order violators become repenting dieters.

Alternatively, lovingly preparing a meal, serving our friends and family in a beautiful environment, and the associated pleasures are a splendid example of a First Order feeling of happiness right alongside the Second Order consequence of good health and the Third Order consequences of connection, love, growth and purpose.

CHILI CHEESE FRIES & BEER

Although not generally acknowledged in circles of fast food haute cuisine, the much-coveted combination of chili cheese fries and beer sit in the pantheon of First Order consequence perpetrators. Their combined nutritional value has the same substantive content as yellowcake (concentrated uranium). This being the case, why are they available and consumed on such a regular basis? The answer is refreshingly simple as the gluttonous chili cheese fries are tasty and fun.

"Wow," she exclaims, as another dose of chili cheese fries passes her lips, "these are delicious and yes, I'll have another beer!" One doesn't need to be endowed with a higher intelligence to know that this food is unhealthy, and yet the immediate gratification, social acceptability and ease of acquisition will thwart any fleeting thoughts of the negative impact on one's health. To further elaborate on the effects of a diet of fast food and the Second and Third Order consequences of its epidemic consumption, note the following fun facts:

1. One in three Americans is fat, double as many as three decades ago.
2. Obesity is affiliated with a higher risk of heart disease, type two diabetes, osteoarthritis, stroke, and colon, breast and endometrial cancers.
3. The ferries in Puget Sound inflated their seat width from eighteen to twenty inches to take into account room for larger posterior regions.
4. Parker Ambulance in Colorado retrofitted its vehicles with a winch and a plus-size compartment to accommodate patients up to 1,000 pounds in weight.
5. A coffin maker in Indiana now provides double-sized patterns.

The Second Order consequences of healthy eating are being fit, trim, energetic and engaged with life. We seem to ignore this one or we think that one pile of cheese fries and a few beers won't matter. We dismiss the consequences of skipping that one workout and pretend it's not significant.

ROOT-INSTANT GRATIFICATION

The root of all these problems lies in the quest for instant gratification. We're constantly surrounded by and challenged to participate in opportunities and events (both good and bad) of stimulation. If the much touted statement that "the majority of our actions, directly or inadvertently, involve the avoidance of pain or the seeking of pleasure" is true, then it would appear that we are physiologically hardwired to seek immediate resolution/gratification in the majority of our actions.

To overcome this "hardwired" propensity for immediate gratification, we need to plan and we need accountability and a deeper level of consciousness.

SIX HUMAN NEEDS

The definition of the six human needs come from a variety of speakers and authors including Tony Robbins and Keith Cunningham. Every human being has deep needs that must be met to feel that elusive happiness we all desire.

Here's a secret: Find a source for these six needs and you won't have to hunt for happiness—happiness will automatically overcome you.

Everything is driven from the six needs:

SIGNIFICANCE

We want to matter and be relevant. Quite often we spend precious time and energy trying to prove our significance through the acquisition of flashy cars, jewelry, big houses, and trophy spouses/partners we don't really like or love. We spend money and energy showing off to get the approval of people we don't know as a means to disprove our own insecurities and doubts.

The mistake is to seek the approval in others and to create the need for that approval in order to validate your own life. To the degree that you can embrace yourself and your own actions and stop needing social validation, you have the opportunity to create significance within your mind, which is its only true place and source.

LOVE & CONNECTION

We need other people. We need, we desire, we thirst for human connection—and without it we are lost. All the money on earth can never buy true love and connection, though having significant amounts of it will not necessarily repel love and connection. If you want certainty, buy a dog.

If you want loyalty buy a dog.
I bought two just to be certain.

—Al Dunlop

A physical substitute for love and connection will always fail. Cars, alcohol, jets, million dollar bank accounts, etc., are all interesting but cannot—and will never be—deeply fulfilling held alone.

A Note from Damion:

When I went into hiding, to live in the shadows of isolation, I constantly sought connection and companionship with women in a superficial and shallow physical way. I tried to satisfy the need for connection and love, but I never found a true connection, just the First Order immediate proximity satisfaction.

A friend from Canada recently asked me, "During this chaotic, scary collapse, where was your family?"

The question stumped me at first. My immediate reaction was that my family didn't understand me or my life, and a voice in the back of my head said that was for the best—that I should keep the deep, dark truth of my destruction from them.

It wasn't that I didn't think my family would care. I knew they cared about me. They just had no reference, experience or bandwidth to be able to relate to losing millions of dollars and fall from grace all the way down into a muddy ditch. I thought I was keeping it from them to protect them, but really I was trying to protect myself.

Upon reflection, I realized that someone can love you without having any way to support you with logistics. They can always support you with connection and empathy. They may not be able to relate to losing five million bucks, but they can appreciate and know pain with you. My self-prescribed isolation prevented me from feeling their support. In that selfish act of self-loathing and desire for self-preservation, I severed the connections that were blood guaranteed. The Third Order consequences—the ones that reflected my most basic needs as a human being—were devastating.

CERTAINTY

We need to have the feeling of certainty and confidence within our lives in some form. With a million variables influencing every piece of every ingredient of our lives, the idea that we can control everything or much of anything is kind of insane. Total control will not happen.

One of the most commonly perceived forms of certainty is money. This could be a certain amount of income from a job, a quantifiable amount of money in the bank, or a number that brings a sense of peace.

Too often we equate the number to the experience. If I have a million dollars, then I'll be good, happy, safe, secure, done, etc. The problem is that the number is an illusion. No number will ever be enough until you realize that the thing we're really trying to achieve is a state of confidence. Fear will always control us if we're counting on external measurements to provide us with certainty, regardless of what the paystub or the bank balance says.

The way to certainty is through internal truth and faith.

A Note from Christofer:

> I embarked upon a path of reinventing my professional self largely as a result of my desire to have a certain amount of financial certainty. There is an overabundance of dialogue, self-help tapes and noted "experts" whose mantra is to convince us that there is "no real financial certainty"—which perhaps could be true on some esoteric level. I am in agreement with the idea that the ultimate experience of sustainable certainty is found in a deep faith, though having a few hundred thousand dollars in cash can be very helpful in eliminating a wide variety of worries that

might otherwise keep you from achieving that level of faith and consciousness.

VARIETY

Doing something over and over again without any concrete goal or system of improvement can make us numb and ultimately crushes our spirit. If we don't find a productive way to experience variety in our lives, we'll find variety in destructive things.

In the business world, people often sabotage themselves by building a business or career and then just as they start to gain momentum and see success from all the hard work, a shiny penny (something interesting and new) catches their eye. So they jump into that gig or deal and get off track.

Whether it's a new investment, a great new business or network marketing opportunity, it doesn't matter because the result is the same. Every time you see the shiny penny and jump to get it, you leave the line you're in and have to start in the back of the line for your new thing. The processional ripples of your commitment weaken, and you are left to flail about until the next shiny object grabs your attention,

We crave variety and must be conscious to how we're creating and getting it. If we're not conscious, we'll always be at the back of some line, always seeking greener grass and forever frustrated that we're not making progress and finding success.

In *Multiple Streams of Income*, author Robert Allen touts the idea of creating many streams of income from a variety of sources. He's actually endorsing variety to people who largely should not be doing anything of the sort because it's distracting to the one thing they should be focused on. Unfortunately, variety is so sexy and appealing that some people can't help but to chase it. It is also a splendid marketing tool to sell self-help books as people find the idea of multiple streams of income and passive income sexy. It is amazing how many systems exist to sell the dream of never-ending mailbox money that (like clockwork) shows up whilst the recipients sip Mai Tais on the beach.

Though a wonderful system for the selling of books and seminars, it has nothing to do with the real world. The truth is, you can't get rich by fracturing your focus on every other investment you run into, just like you can't have a great romantic relationship if you're constantly distracted by and pursuing every other hot body you encounter. That's a sure fire recipe for disaster. Stop chasing squirrels!

> *Get in line, stay in line.*
> —Keith Cunningham

A Note from Damion:

In years past I found variety in dating lots of different women. Even when I had love and connection, I blew it up by diverting into variety for variety's sake and energetically engaged with other interesting women. This need must have a conscious outlet or your unconscious will create an outlet at the expense of one of your other basic human needs.

GROWTH

We're either growing or dying. The universe doesn't do flat, and neither do humans. If you think, "Hey, I'm good. I can go on cruise control," YOU'RE DYING. Focus on expanding your mind. Engage, learn, study and connect.

The principle of entropy says that anything that doesn't get constant energy and care will die through atrophy. Human beings are no different. Growth is not just stashing more money in a bank account or getting bigger muscles. Growth is the expansion of truth and moving into a higher state of mastery in all things, from relationships to finance, from an amazing lifestyle to super parenting.

A Note from Damion:

Here's a question: Have you ever been really unhappy and growing at the same time? It's doubtful. Back in the time before my reinvention, in the days when I was in a state of perpetual fear, I was dying. I was not growing and for that matter I wasn't even conscious to the problem. I was so busy hiding from everything, everyone and the truth I didn't even realize part of the way out of the fear was to start growing again.

Today both of us (Christofer and I) are growing in all sorts of ways—expanding our mind with TED talks, reading powerful books, studying self-improvement seminars, practicing yoga, meditating daily, traveling to new and foreign lands, meeting and engaging with amazing people, seeking to grow capital and creating businesses that do good, and on and on. We're both conscious of putting ourselves in growth spaces, and you should be too! As long as we consciously find ways to grow, in large part the growth, by default, keeps us in a state of bliss, happiness and joy.

Ask yourself, what can you do today to grow? Now take that first step! It will change everything and bring you into the present moment, raising your consciousness immediately.

CONTRIBUTION

Ways to contribute are endless. It could be supporting a foundation, the Rotary, or a charity to which you donate time or money. It could be writing a book, posting on a blog, mentoring a child or another person, or even building a legacy that will be shared for generations.

The point of contribution is to take part in something that is greater than yourself and lives beyond you. What is larger than you and will keep receiving the benefit(s) of your contribution after you aren't here anymore? The answer to this will lead towards contribution. Ask the question and consider what your life would be if you felt contribution.

For type A personalities, we tend to need to be around oceans, mountains, big things because they're much bigger than us and we're inspired by their sheer magnitude. Creating value that lives beyond you will serve you no matter what personality type you are, but it's especially important for the achiever crowd.

Contribution will put you into an energy of purpose. It's highly unlikely you'll feel a lack of purpose or feel stuck in life while you're in the process of contributing. You'll be present and in all likelihood find a great deal of inner peace through conscious contribution.

WELLNESS

It's the truth: If you don't have your health, you don't have anything. Ironically, people spend the first part of their lives sacrificing their health to accumulate as much money as they can, only to spend the last part of their lives using all that money to get their health back. How does this make any rational sense?

Look around and watch people. Listen to them, maybe even listen to yourself. The conversation goes something like this: "I feel like garbage. I need to lose thirty pounds. I'm tired. I'm not happy with my body, health, wellness." Meanwhile, Twinkies, pizza, beers, fried junk, and processed crap continue to slide down their gullet. Then they find every reason to watch football instead of going outside to play football, get a workout, take a Yoga class, exercise, etc.

PASSION

Passion isn't something you find; it's a derivative of growth and contribution. Deep down we want passion in our love lives, our careers, and our health—even though we destroy it in the process of demanding it be fulfilled immediately.

Passion must be earned.

How often have you heard this (or said it yourself—admit it, both of us have!):

- "If I could just find my passion, I'd be happy."
- "My spouse doesn't do it for me. He's so boring. I want and need someone to excite me!"
- "My career is lame. If I could just find the thing I'm passionate about, I'd be successful."

The constant here, there, everywhere is projection of the problem. The problem is *always* within ourselves. We create it. But in a way, that's actually good news. It means we have the opportunity to solve it! Whatever we choose to engage in, we can engage in it with reckless abandon.

We engage our lives full on. We engage our spouse as if we've never known another person and this is our one and only chance to connect with another human being. We engage in our chosen business with the belief that it is the only opportunity we'll ever have for contribution, for wealth, or for money.

We engage until we know it's time to disengage, and then we pull the brake cord and get off the train. What we don't do is continue on with a feeble attempt to ride multiple trains and play the "grass is greener" game. This ends badly. Always has, always will.

DAMION'S STORY

MONEY

In the height of my fear, I created a powerful and superficial "still got my AMEX Black card" persona so people I didn't even know would continue to validate me with looks of, "Wow! You must be important with that celebrity card!" I remember one of my dear friends asking me if I still had my Black card during the time I was melting down and losing everything. I whipped it out and proudly said, "Oh yeah, still got the big boy card!" He smiled and gave me a high five and cheers.

I could have found significance and validation for myself in the truth if I was conscious. The comfort of finding immediate but temporary (First Order) significance from the surface-level validation from others, whether I knew them or not, was the primary motivation for all my actions. I was still going through my accumulation period where the status quo continued to exist so long as I ignored the truth, kept consuming and continued spending. The damage to my soul kept compounding until the strutting peacock could strut no longer.

For years I had embarked on a "build-up period," a time where I was singularly focused on acquiring more. More money, more toys, more women, more stuff. The higher I built my pile of stuff, the more significance I convinced myself I had until I suffocated myself beneath all that insignificant garbage.

I thought if I could just get more money I'd be happy so I got more money. I satisfied the First Order consequence that money meant power and freedom. Getting more meant I was all set! At least that's what I thought. I built spreadsheets that proved it. They told me once I hit $2 million that I'd have $200,000 in passive income to retire on and live the rest of my life in bliss. Once I had the $2 million, I'd be done. Cash was the answer, so I thought.

And so I went out into the world, tried a few things, landscaping, banking, insurance and then real estate. All flops until real estate, when I found a shortcut to get the money. This gave me the tool I needed to get all of the creature comforts and the instant satisfaction I'd always wanted. I saw the way to $2 million and my First Order consequences were conquered!

I remember receiving $5,000, $10,000 and even $25,000 checks in my first year in real estate for a single "thing" I did. I'd made it! The problem was that I was so focused on the immediate harvest that I didn't think about the following month or year or decade. I didn't think about the long-term consequences of my thoughts and patterns. I didn't think about the Second and Third Order consequences of my choices and decisions at all.

I was making money, and I was spending money. I was hunting and killing the deals, but I wasn't planting trees that would mature over time, with deep and strong roots. I wasn't building up a genuine satisfaction in what I was doing that would survive the droughts and fires of economic cycles.

The deep need for certainty was elusive because I focused on making big chunks of cash. Although I was buying assets that actually could have produced long-term certainty, I quickly harvested each asset, either selling it or leveraging it with new debt, etc. Any long-term certainty and security was killed before it had the chance to naturally bloom into a money tree. *The deals were never the problem. I was always the problem.*

Comparing then and now, I've fallen in love with the process and the cause, not the effect. I'm building assets of creation, using my brain and my integrity to create value for other people. These assets, born of ideas, are endless. Finding a certainty in $200,000 of annual passive income has become irrelevant. I don't have to rely on numbers or things to give me security or purpose.

I'm focused on bringing value to other people, and the rewards continue to arrive as I stay involved and focused on the sharing and the giving, not the consolidating and taking, which in large part had been my modus operandi in the pre-reinvention days.

LOVE

As far as relationships go, my belief was that if I could just find the perfect girl I'd be happy. I kept "trying out" the flavor of the month. I would find reasons each of them was wrong, flawed, inept at keeping up, or simply not at my level. I made them wrong in my mind. I made myself right in my mind. I was never the problem…except, of course, I was the problem.

Reinventing myself in this arena meant diving deep past the First Order consequences. First Order thinking: "Wow, she's beautiful, I want to be close to her and take her home, woo and win her." I started asking myself how the Second Order consequences could be met: the feelings of being deeply loved and able to love another, not just the chemical lust of a new conquest.

I asked, "How can I love and cherish another?" Instead of asking how to find the perfect person, I asked, "How can I become the best version of me that would naturally attract this person?" And when I asked different questions, the results started showing up totally different.

Challenging myself to be better and more honest—as opposed to desperately seeking to conquer and manage others—pushed the fear away and brought a peace. When manipulation and orchestration faded into participation and acceptance, love was automatic and everywhere.

In terms of Third Order consequences, *i.e.*, my need for love and connection, the relationships I've formed since the reinvention bristle with love and connection. I've never felt so much love and connection being projected outward or coming at me from those I'm with. When I focused on changing myself and being honest, loving, compassionate and genuinely present, a different type of person started showing up (starting with me) and the relationships were totally different. They were interesting, connected, satisfying and without anxiety. The need to find the next one while in the current one evaporated completely.

This doesn't mean I haven't met and engaged with a few "misses" where there was no real connection. Regardless of how conscious I become, I'm as capable of doing dumb things and making mistake as anyone else.

The big difference today, now that I'm driven by and engaged in the truth of "what is," is that I recognize when I am in a dud situation and it's time to move on. This recognition happens easily and quickly. I value myself and other people more than I value trying to force anything or make the wrong person happy, including myself.

HEALTH

For over a decade, all throughout my twenties, I focused on making money and living large. I had low self-esteem, and one way I validated my significance was through overindulging in food and drink. I satisfied my connection need through food and drink. I satisfied part of my variety need through food and drink. I fooded and drinked myself into a fat, out-of-shape, unhealthy man.

Every time I'd order the deluxe Sea Bass smothered in butter, a second martini, the cheesecake, and the chili fries, I told myself, "Yeah, you're worth it, you earned it, you're significant!" My First Order need was fulfilled, and I never looked beyond it. Many times the food and drink experiences gave me an opportunity to connect with people. I used that connection as an excuse to try more new versions of consumption, regardless of the long-term impact on my body of all this gluttony. Ultimately, this pattern pushed me over two-hundred pounds and into a form I was embarrassed to look at in the mirror.

The mirror was showing me a body in line with my bloated, unhealthy mind and soul.

After my trigger event, one moment of clarity came to me in the fall of 2010 when I received an email from a friend who'd lost over a hundred pounds in less than six months through conscious eating and a rigid exercise program. In one moment I decided to course correct, and 120 days later I'd shed the excess by going conscious and developing new patterns and habits of eating and working out. I wrote down every morsel of food, every calorie, every drink I sipped, and I went to the gym regardless of how tired I was, six days a week.

My Second Order consequential needs crushed my immediate desire for gooey cheese fries. My Third Order needs were satisfied by the connections I found in the community of people also transforming their physical health. I found connection through support and engagement with them. I stopped spending time with those chili-cheese-fry-eating losers I'd been drawn to.

I started seeking out variety through new exotic healthy foods at Whole Foods or Raw and at organic restaurants. To my surprise they were everywhere. I didn't realize they were all around me until I had this awakening, when my mind shifted into the truth of health and I went conscious. At the point I found alignment between the three levels of consequence in my mind, happiness happened. I engaged health and noticed it all around me—wow, how interesting!

QUESTIONS & ACTIONS

1. List three areas in which you consistently seek and obtain immediate gratification though know the pursuit and outcome is destructive.
2. What is the period of time it will take (in your estimation) to achieve their acquisition? Are you aware of the price you will need to pay (good or bad) to obtain them? Are you okay with the price you think you will need to pay to get them?
3. List 3 areas in which you have a goal of creating something that you greatly value though do not need immediately.
4. If you look at the part of your life that you want to reinvent/change, what is one thing you do that might be getting in the way of your bigger goal? Can you change it or do you need assistance?

5. Do you think that you can have whatever you want in this life? If so, why don't you all of these things, experiences etc. now? With all of the things that you want in item 3, do you know the specific process of obtaining them? If so, list the steps. If not, why are they on your list?

5

SUCCESS VS. FULFILLMENT

Happiness comes when your work and words are of benefit to yourself and others.

—The Buddha

def.

Success

1. The accomplishment of an aim or purpose.
2. The attainment of social status or profit.
3. The opposite of failure.

THEORY

Failure is the state or condition of not meeting a desirable or intended objective, and may be viewed as the opposite of success. Product failure can range from failure to sell to product malfunction, in the worst cases leading to personal injury, the province of forensic engineering.

Ironically, someone who fails to achieve a certain objective is often seen as a failure although the greatest successes have been those who "failed" first, often repeatedly.

Our 21st century Western culture is obsessed about the trappings of success and being successful. Everywhere we see tokens of this obsession, symbols that prove how successful we are to the world. The bigger house, the shiny things, the Gucci purse, the Jimmy Choo shoes, the Italian cars, the prestigious "vice president" title are just a few of the myriad of this type of "success." Success many times means more money, more glamour, more power. Inevitably it means more of *something* to most people. The constant focus on being successful is an illusion because the bar is ever-growing as others are constantly playing the same game. It's never-ending, with the deeper (Third Order) need for fulfillment lost in the tokens and status symbols of success.

One of our mentors, Keith Cunningham, suggests we focus on mastery instead of success. The journey into mastery is the journey into the essence of something. In our experience, having mastery means being humble enough that you never need to prove it, you simply embody it.

Martial arts typify the distinction between success and mastery (a driver of fulfillment). For example: Getting a black belt has absolutely nothing to do with being a black belt. Getting a black belt is as simple as going to Google and ordering a black-colored belt from a martial arts supply store. Now you've got a black belt. On the other hand, *being* a black belt is a shift in awareness. It's an awakening to the abilities and instinctive movements that come from endless distinctions and practice as you narrow down the tolerances for the slightest movements.

When I was invited to take my black belt test in 2004, I remember being excited and feeling nervous at first. My Sensei Brian Vickery, himself a 4th degree black belt in Aikido, looked at me and said, "Damion, you're already a black belt. Just go out and have fun demonstrating who you are. You know the movements. You're already Shodan (the name of the first degree black belt).” I didn't totally understand what this meant back then, but I understand today. It's interesting to note that someone who becomes a black belt isn't necessarily a master of the art. Rather, the black belt is the recognition of becoming a dedicated student and a recognition of being.

What art are you a dedicated student of?

MEDIOCRITY

One of the reasons people find so much joy in their hobbies and would rather be fishing, golfing, skiing, playing or anything except “work” is often because they're not a dedicated student of their art. Once you change minds and live in the space, a focus on mastery becomes more and more fulfilling as a product of the growth that occurs when you focus on intelligent practice.

If you're focused on the ends (the success event), you'll never live a fulfilled life because the end event usually moves further and further away. In the unlikely event you hit that end event, you're immediately pushed to aim and strive for more. Our entire societal framework beats into us that more is better. If you're happy with what you've got, then somehow something is wrong with you. There's always something more to obtain, another item you're lacking, another status symbol just out of reach. It's a never-ending “success” loop that can't be completed. We're trained and pushed to never be satisfied.

The following exchange in the movie *Wall Street 2* between Shia LeBeouf and Josh Brolin encapsulates this ingrained belief system:

LeBeouf: "What's your number? The amount of money you'd need to walk away from it and just live. See I find that everybody has a number, and it's usually an exact number, so what is yours?"

Brolin: "More."

Success is focused on what you can get; fulfillment is about you can give. In the process of reinvention you have to change your mind and move from the context of getting to giving. Your questions will evolve from asking, "Can I do this?" to "Should I do this?" The questions become more powerful as you ask questions of fulfillment and avoid those of success.

You'll move away from asking *how* to get something and towards asking *why* you're doing something. The cycle of never-endingly chasing success is diametrically opposed to our First Order desire for everything to be easier and faster. In the battle of success versus fulfillment, we're lazy, impatient and greedy.

But what about the lawyer or doctor or business person who worked twenty hours a day for ten years to become successful? How are they lazy, greedy or impatient? If they were focused on being a successful professional, they were likely working as little as they had to, even if that was twenty hours a day, to achieve their vision of what success looked like. They pursued the shortest route to the most money and took shortcuts whenever they could.

In the pursuit of mastery and fulfillment you have a deep sense of purpose, even if you don't know what the end is. Your growth creates fulfillment, and the "end event" (your vision of what success looks like) stops being your sole focus. In fact, in the deepest sense of mastery, there is no end; there are only finer and finer distinctions.

DAMION'S STORY

FERRARI 550

One of my favorite movies in my twenties was *Bad Boys 2*. I watched it dozens of times. I loved the adrenaline, and I loved the car Will Smith drove. Part of my mind got ahold of the idea that having that same titanium Ferrari would make me Will Smith, a badass stud who was highly significant and super successful.

Once I'd put that car on my dream board and listed it in my goals, it was a matter of time before it was in my garage. In 2005, as my cash was peaking (in large part because of my ability to borrow ridiculous amounts of money), I ordered the car, and I got that car.

Debt gave me the illusion of wealth, but a dollar borrowed is not a dollar earned.

I'd convinced myself I was doing better the more I could borrow. Optimism is the enemy of wealth and borrowing for consumption is the cousin! When I got the American Express Black Card, I could project success with my unlimited celebrity metal charge card. And because of my insecurity, I used this to spend money in ridiculous ways in amounts that made me shake my head in disbelief. During my reinvention period I switched to cash and stopped buying things I couldn't pay for as I consumed them. This was a different experience, and interestingly enough, stress seemed to dissipate as a result of implementing this habit.

Before my reinvention, the continuing desire to find fulfillment through successfully gathering satisfaction from outside events went on for years. I worked on opening a restaurant but ended up with a half-built shell—sort of a good analogy of me at the time. I launched a network-marketing career, building a network of several thousand people in less than six months, only to have the compensation plan revamped and my $10,000 a month in expected income obliterated. I sought satisfaction across the country while volunteering on a political campaign where I eventually got fired—yeah, fired—from a volunteer position.

So long as I sought external successes, it mattered not what form they took—they were all and always the same. They were momentarily interesting and satisfying until the First Order pleasure faded and they became just another shiny toy that gets boring the day after Christmas.

In the reinvention process, I let go of trying to control what manmade fulfillment would look like and picking the perfect external "thing" to be successful in. My new mind insisted on true fulfillment, not success. Success was a byproduct, fulfillment was the practice.

I found fulfillment was part of me having intention towards mastery and service. To the degree in which I was focused on servicing with greater transparency and greater improvement of other people's lives through whatever I was doing, I was flushed with joy and fulfillment. It got to the point where I only go to bed because I'm falling asleep mid-sentence writing or creating more value for the world in the projects I take on.

Fulfillment is a natural byproduct of being in relationships that inspire and elevate all the parties. Whether it's the clients I choose to work with or the friends I hang out with, we're in a shared space of trust and mutual growth. I'm no longer a pitchman in business. I'm a trusted advisor and serving people, never selling them.

Today I'm asked to advise and be part of world-class people's trusted teams because I'm valuable and trusted. A totally different type of person wants to be in friendship with me, someone who wants to grow and expand into their true potential. The ones I engage with know I'm on that course, too. And in that mind together, we chart amazing waters. It's in this field of fulfillment that I live and exist. I will never go back to a success-focused life or mind; it's a brutal illusion that will suck the soul juice from your spirit so long as success is the primary driver over fulfillment.

HIGHER EDUCATION TOKENS

I recently watched *Finding Joe*, one of the best movies on purpose and truth I've ever seen. In the movie Brian Johnson, the founder of "Philosophers Notes," tells the story of dropping out of law school in his first year and how people told him to stick with it even though it made him nauseous. The belief that we'll be seen as successful and automatically jump up the social later when we earn a degree or two is a powerful and prevalent force in society, all over the world. Fortunately for Brian and the world, he quit and pursued his bliss.

Even after all that I've been through, the companies I've built, and the experiences I've had, I still in my own life had the drive to get a degree a couple years ago and so enrolled at the University of Texas. I had all sorts of reasons to enroll, from getting the degree in case I ran for office to the social connections of being on the Board of Regents someday and even season tickets to the football games here in Austin. I enrolled full time in the fall of 2011 and lasted one single class.

I was angry, sick, lost and annoyed almost every minute of that single forty-five-minute class. When I walked outside after class and sat down on a bench to contemplate the future, I realized I was there to satisfy the getting of an educational success token. The token had nothing to do with fulfillment. I learned a valuable lesson in this process. Inadvertently this was the fourth time I'd gone to college for all the wrong reasons. The lesson I learned was that the truth is inside me, and when I give into social pressures to prove my worth to other people, I'll find myself lacking fulfillment even if I achieve "success" via a new token. I'll be living out other people's needs, not mine, and in doing this I'll be living a lie.

What lie might you be living today, something that you are doing or choosing that goes against your truth but satisfies what you think someone else wants?

TRUE PURPOSE

How many times have you heard people around you, close friends, maybe even yourself, struggle to find the true purpose of their life? We've heard it so many times we've lost count. It may be one of the biggest struggles for human beings, ever. People have this misguided belief that once they find their true purpose everything will be better. I actually think my previous self thought my purpose was to make a ton of money in real estate and live large. I succeeded but was miserable. The purpose of my life was unlikely that.

Today I'm convinced our true purpose will not be known until after we're gone. That's not to say that we have to stumble around aimlessly until we die. All we have to do is pay attention to the taps on the shoulder we get from the universe. Buckminster Fuller called this "precession." As we move along in life, we'll get feedback—taps—and they'll either be supportive or they'll be warnings.

We can tell by the supportive taps that we're on the path we're supposed to be on. This is called the "flow." You've felt this at one time or another. The feeling and knowledge that things are clicking, stuff is happening, you've got momentum, and your thing is effortless. This feedback is the universe supporting your movement of what you're doing.

Don't look for your purpose in front of you. If you're looking ahead, you're not seeing your purpose but your outcome (desired goal). Instead, look for your purpose to be travelling along right beside you. *Because purpose is something you can engage in right now, not later when you're a "success."* You don't have to reach purpose. You just have to follow along with it.

If you're travelling in the wrong direction, your purpose won't be there next to you. Unfortunately, it's not always easy to see your purpose because even when it's right next to you, it's often in your blind spot. That's why taps and signs from the universe are so important. You'll be able to tell when you're travelling with purpose, not away from it.

A great example is money. If you're aligned with your purpose and traveling in the right direction, money takes care of itself as a byproduct. But if you focus on all the money ahead of you and treat it as if it's your purpose in life, the offshoot will not be fulfillment. Instead, it may be rather gruesome like my life was before my reinvention when my focus was on cash, cash, cash.

THE PARABLE OF THE HONEYBEE

The honeybee is a good example of purpose. The honeybee goes to the flower to get nectar to make honey, but as he's buzzing around between flowers, he is also cross-pollinating all the flowers and supporting the entire system, unbeknownst to the bee. His purpose is travelling alongside his motion, the same as ours.

Listen to the taps you get from the universe. If you notice negative tap after negative tap, consider them to be warnings. Too often those taps are misinterpreted as hurdles that we're supposed to overcome. The more conscious you are, the more clearly you'll see the difference between a huddle and a warning sign.

Fuller had this to say about true purpose: "Your significance will forever remain a mystery but will unfold if your highest purpose is your dedication to the highest advantage of others."

QUESTIONS & ACTIONS

1. When you write down your goals, what percentage of your goals are about "stuff" as opposed to experiences?
2. If you knew you could not "fail" and that your worse nightmare would never come true, what would you be doing right now?
3. When you look around at what you want in your life, do you think about all of the things, people, and stuff you want to conquer or do you think more about the things you wish to contribute? What is your focus?

6
STILLNESS

def.

The state or instance of being quiet or calm.

> *The stillness in stillness is not the real stillness; only when there is stillness in movement does the universal rhythm manifest.*

> —Bruce Lee

Through return to simple living comes control of desires. In control of desires stillness is attained. In stillness the world is restored.

—Lao Tzu

Within you there is a stillness and a sanctuary to which you can retreat at any time and be yourself.

—Hermann Hesse

It has often occurred to me that a seeker after truth has to be silent.

—Gandhi

Be soft in your practice. Think of the method as a fine silvery stream, not a raging waterfall. Follow the stream, have faith in its course. It will go its own way, meandering here, trickling there. It will find the grooves, the cracks, the crevices. Just follow it. Never let it out of your sight. It will take you…

—Sheng-yen

THEORY

When we find quiet, when we are quiet, we have the ability to ask questions and to find peace. Have you ever been at the ocean by yourself where all you hear is waves and your thoughts? Ever been in the woods and all you hear is the rustling of leaves and the birds chirping, plus your thoughts? What about when your eyes are closed and all you hear is your breath and your thoughts? In these moments of stillness, the truth can engulf you and peace can find you.

The world is speeding up and getting noisier by the second. As long as we join the world in this chaotic, loud entanglement, we'll be lost, anxious and rarely in the truth. If we happen to bump into the truth, it may be for such a short moment that we won't even notice it or we'll think, "Wow, cool!" and then crash into more noise. The noise is what suffocates our spirit, and the noise is what we must let go of if we're to shift and reinvent our life. Noise keeps us stuck and distracted. Peace, quiet and stillness create transparency and clarity of vision on what is true.

DAMION'S STORY

YOGA

Finding the truth is the cornerstone of any reinvention. In 2010, after I moved to Austin, Christofer casually told me how yoga allows him to open his body to fully meditate. At the time I didn't think much of it, but it changed everything for me within a year.

Fast forward to fall of 2011. I'm with Deepak Chopra in Carlsbad, California. He tells me that the truth of the Universe, God, everything shows up in the space between our thoughts. I give it a shot and open up into mediation after yoga. BOOM. A fire hose of truth knocks me over.

When I'm busy talking, telling and proving myself, I'm blocking the truth and the valve to the fire hose is clamped off. But when I quieted the mind to observe the flow of thoughts, I asked myself if, in that moment, I was comfortable with who I was. The resounding "ohmmmmm" answer was clear: I was in truth and at peace. At that moment, the chatter on the internet, blogospheres and even behind my back became powerless to affect my thoughts, mind and being.

Prior to that moment, I gave great power to what others said about me. A lot of what had bothered me on the interest had pieces of truth and was embarrassing. I remember reading the comments on a picture of me and a Lamborghini I was test driving. The chatter was all about one of my new Italian cars and I remember being upset that people were creating stories. The fascinating truth was that I was doing the same thing: making up stories about how amazing I was vis-á-vis the shiny metal toys I was playing with. The internet bloggers were in sync with my storytelling, and it made me mad!

The judgments on the internet were an attack, but instead of asking myself what part of the judgment was correct or what piece was bugging me (because it was true), I went straight into the fight, defending and denying. My popular strategy was to call someone crazy or just ignore them altogether, clearly a very mature approach.

I was yearning to find significance for myself in these things—the flashy and the sexy. Today, if I decided to drive a Ferrari or buy a new Porsche, I'd be doing it for me and for the experience it would bring me, not because I'm trying to prove anything or hide behind it to cover for my insecurities. Whatever might be written about me and/or a car today would have zero power over me, the opposite of 2006.

FEAR VS. FAITH

True freedom is the ability to make choices based on values, rather than choosing out of fear or guilt. Free people make commitments because they feel it's the right thing to do, and they are wholehearted about it. Responsibility for your actions isn't a chore or a curse; instead, it means you're reaping the good you sow in keeping your relationships healthy and loving—as well as being able to say no to things you shouldn't be responsible for.

SEVERING OLD CONNECTIONS

During my reinvention, one of the biggest tests came from my old self (the old mind) trying to stay connected to past relationships established during the dark ages, the time when I was in hiding. In the dark ages I was always casting lures for connection, a lure effective at hooking women in mass.

Fast forward to 2012, and I'm still busy experiencing the desire for connection. But I'm no longer drawn to the connections of the past. The people I knew in the past are largely still in the same mind they were back then, while I've taken on a new mind and a completely different presence.

The old me still pops up every now and again, trying to become relevant by reaching out to the past and pulling me into the old entanglements. The old mind is still trying its same old trick, the only trick it knows—lying. And my current mind has no interest in those lies or those old relationships. But the desperate, hiding, longing little boy mind of 2008 wants very much to keep close to those bodies who were part of his survival.

I realize in writing this how the different pieces of us—the stillness me of today versus chaotic me of 2008—are always in conflict, like the vampires and the werewolves in *Twilight*. The contest for supremacy never ends.

In 2008 the dark part of me suffocated the truth, keeping me on edge, constantly juggling relationships, and focusing on external connections for validation of being worthy of being. My value as a human being had such little power or relevance in my dark mind I barely knew it was there. It was devastating and painful.

In a self-fulfilling maneuver my dark side created a representation of me that created connections with others and maintained those connections in all sorts of ways—mostly inauthentic relative to my truth, but totally authentic in relation to my dark side, the scared, hiding me. The connections I made were maintained as long as I kept up the dance of the dark. I was "loved" by the people my representative was connected to as long as I maintained the lies.

Fear of losing my connection to these people kept me from the truth until the lies and the darkness eventually blew up into a trigger event and the movement into the light and truth.

The saying that light is the great sanitizer is powerful and true. The more light I shined on my life, on who I was in relation to others and inside, the more I was disgusted and the more the mind of truth gained power and energy. As I removed layer upon layer of lie and deceit, I found deeper meaning in my human value and a calming sense of peace. The commotion and noise fled because it had no power.

Then one day it happened. I pulled out the sword and slayed my connections to the past, not to hurt the others but to truly and completely let them go. Said another way, I severed my old mind's grip on the connections and opened the door and space for my mind of today to connect with other people in truth, not in desperation.

I made the decision to live in the light and truth and not in the shadows and lies. Thus I'm only going to be in relationships and share my life and space with people and ideas who choose to join this mind, this me. The links between others and the former mind, the former me, no longer get power. They are no longer relevant, and they no longer serve a valid purpose.

The realization that my fear-based mind of old was still hoping for a seat at the table in 2012 and still desired a connection with those people from the bygone era slammed into me in the shower one day, almost knocking me over. I literally ran to my pen and paper, half-covered in soap, with the truth rushing hard and fast through my brain, looking for a destination. I didn't want to lose the lesson or the essence of what just surfaced in a surprise moment of clarity.

Desperation creates noise and a need for control. Honesty calms the movement and noise and allows for a deeper stillness than one can ever imagine until coming into it. To reinvent yourself into a new mind, a new you, you have to find a new mind able to let go of the past. My past relationships didn't serve my present or my future unless I wanted to keep the devious part of me empowered. That was who had those connections—the old me, not the true me of today.

At one point I found myself in conflict with some of the people of pre-reinvention days. I was sharing the current truth and was rebuffed, pushed back and felt anger and pain from them.

CONSISTENCY

I get it. They want the old Damion, the guy that was the dancer, the representative, the Ferrari-driving, smooth-talking life of the party. When I sit in silence or look at them with eyes of truth, the contrast from the old me couldn't be starker and it scares the living hell out of most of them. We've all held on to past links to serve insecurities about the uncertainty of today. But my mind today is perfectly certain that these past entanglements are toxic and automatically repels them because of the decision to move into a different space, the space of truth.

When you reinvent your life, you have to choose your connections. You have to choose what makes sense for the mind you're going to operate from. The choice will be obvious when you shift your mind, but it won't be easy because your old mind will still clamor for relevance. It will test you and try to gain traction. It will want the old stimuli—the old things, people, feelings—and you'll have to decide over and over every time it tries to take control.

You'll have to ask, "Who am I going to be? Am I the previous me or am I the me that sees and lives the truth with greater light and clarity?"

What was true for you in the past was based on your reality, the perceptions and environments. It was true then, just as what you perceive today is true today. You'll perceive and understand different truths tomorrow, and ultimately the reinvention process will continue on as long as you wish to grow and evolve into your higher self.

FULL POTENTIAL

The question you really need to ask is, "Do I wish to become everything I should be? Or do I wish to be part of what I can in the moment?"

Human beings are the only species with the ability to choose to live up to a partial potential. The emotions and mind of a human will ask, "Can I do something?" only for fear and all sorts of influences to answer back with a resounding "No!" Nowhere else in nature do we see an animal ask if they can do something. They simply do what they have the ability to do and no less.

If anything, they ask, "Should I?" (such as a dog wondering if it should steal food from the table). A dog doesn't ask if it can protect its family; it simply jumps in and does so when the need arises. Fear and doubt never enter into it. A dog will never talk itself out of doing what it was meant to do. Likewise, a tree doesn't stop growing once it reaches five feet in height if it's supposed to grow to fifty. It grows because it can and it should and it has the potential to do so. A pride of lions will produce as many offspring as it has the ability to do, and each lion will fight to the death to protect its family. It does this because it has the ability to do so and it should do so.

Humans stop before we're done and use one of our minds to validate that it's okay to stop short. If you wish to reinvent, part of you must be the oak tree or the lion and continue to stay in motion. You must stay in motion because you have the ability and because your motion is part of your potential. That doesn't mean you should go buy a Ferrari or a yacht just because you can figure out a way to finance it or you've got the millions to do it. Part of the human experience is to decide if you should, and the mind of truth gives you all the feedback you need to make this decision. Clarity comes when you move into stillness and open up to what is.

What does all this mean? It means the only way to find stillness (which is where you'll find the truth) is to take responsibility for absolutely everything and I mean everything. I can already hear your mind, "But I didn't have anything to do with my uncle abusing me, I didn't cause the recession, I didn't, I didn't, I didn't... He did it, they did it..." So my question is, how can anything change if you aren't the one running it?

Here's the answer: You have the ability to create meaning from it.

When the financial meltdown happened in 2008, millions of dollars suddenly vanished. All the big-money real estate investors (including me!—Damion) stock brokers, mortgage brokers etc., spent the next few years telling themselves and anyone else who would listen that they didn't cause the recession. No individual person was in charge of the economy so no one in particular was responsible. They all shifted to blame and justification. Everyone was at the mercy of the economy and endless things outside their control.

THE MELTDOWN

My reinvention happened only when I took responsibility for one hundred percent of what happened to me economically. I own both my role in the meltdown—which includes how I set deals up, how I managed the finances, how I interacted with people, presented myself, etc.—and I own the meaning I give the meltdown, including all of the lawsuits, credit collapse, upset investors, angry lovers, etc.

This didn't happen right after my trigger event. It took years. For a long time, I refused responsibility for things that happened when my old mind was in control.

As soon as I took responsibility for me, I didn't have to fix the stuff, the people, the projects from five years ago. I gave myself the grace to be human and mess up. I allowed for that experience to be true. In the past, before reinvention, I was very busy managing and manipulating the "truth" to explain away my old self as good Damion vs. egomaniac Damion.

When I took responsibility, I realized I had acted the part of a real arrogant bastard and had surrounded myself with the type of people who would connect with an arrogant bastard. I learned that arrogance attracts certain people and humility attracts others. A great example is the rebel in school that gets the hot girlfriend and the nice guy who goes home alone. The nice guy can't figure out why he can't get the hot girl, but that's really the wrong question. The question he should ask is, "Do I want to act like the rebel and attract that kind of girl, or do I want to maintain my integrity and share space with those who connect with true me?"

We can open the door to sharing with others or we can manipulate, manage and change ourselves to be more attractive to certain people. Women constantly do this strutting to make themselves into an illusion that's attractive to guys. They work on creating a version of themselves that's all done up and exudes sexiness until they nab the guy they want, and then they shift into frumpy blobs and wonder why their guy's losing interest. It's because they never let the guy see the true them, only the illusion—so it's no wonder the guy was only interested in the illusion, not the person.

Guys do the same crap. Guys will court and woo the ladies until she falls for him, and then the guy goes, "Hey, I won! The game is done!" Then he shifts back to the natural version of himself— the honest, non-courting version—and the woman wonders where her man went.

STILLNESS IN LOVE

Men and women are giving up on each other more quickly and easily than ever before. We're giving up more and more on the value of being in relationship and fully engaging with another person.

Men are more and more often seeking stimulus online, either instantly or through shallow entanglements. They're trying to skip out on the drama, pain and noise of fully engaging, but they're also missing out on the deeper connection and peace from a loving relationship. A form of true stillness lies in the peace shared with one's partner.

Women are more accepting of the belief that they don't need men, that men just want sex, that men are pigs. They'll say, "What's the point?" when they can accomplish all their goals without depending on an another, unpredictable, undependable person. Besides with all the stress they're under, who needs to deal with the needs of a man?

Both men and women are so busy succeeding and satisfying all of the First Order desires and goals that they're missing the entire point of stillness and connection with another person, a true partner. They're missing one of the most fulfilling opportunities we're blessed with given this human experience thing we're in.

THROWAWAY SOCIETY

Ultimately, this dynamic of a throwaway society, the me first society, plays out over and over until we find stillness and take responsibility for everything in our life. It continues until we reinvent our being at the core and how we operate. Until we reinvent completely we're bound to go through these cycles in shifting forms indefinitely. We're bound to continue stuck in the circle until we have a trigger event or die in perpetual rotation.

When you own it all, that is, when you take responsibility for everything in your life, you shift into a place of consciousness and power that enables you to let go of anything at anytime. Until you own it all, it owns you and you are powerless to change anything.

QUESTIONS & ACTIONS

1. Do you practice/experience stillness in your life and, if so, how and where?
2. Meditate for ten minutes a day. Step one, sit on the floor in a quiet room. Step two, close your eyes. Step three, listen to your breath for ten minutes.
3. Take a yoga and Aikido class. Sign up NOW!

7

THE RUNWAY

def.

1. A leveled strip of smooth ground along which aircraft take off and land.
2. The area or path along which a jumper, pole vaulter, or javelin thrower runs.

def. (as it relates to a career/job/company reinvention)

The financial resources combined with a specific time-bounded plan to initiate and tacticly prove a process of career or job reinvention.

THEORY

...BUT FIRST, A SLIGHT DIGRESSION INTO AVIATION METAPHORS

As a pilot, two of the most critical items on a preflight checklist are calculating weight & balance and fuel consumption. Not getting the weight and center of gravity (CG) correct can result in a number of performance issues (assuming you get airborne) ranging from increased fuel burn or, in an extreme case, crashing.

The pilot must take into consideration the aforementioned payload as well as the aircraft's vector (course), flight time, distance to destination, fuel consumption, average speed, and altitude, and then do his best to foresee any events (weather, etc.) that might appear without warning during the flight.

So in summary, if the plane is carrying too much stuff (payload) and the pilot did not correctly plan his fuel requirements, there's a good chance the aircraft will not make it to its intended destination and in a worst case it may actually crash.

UNDERSTANDING AND DESIGNING YOUR REINVENTION RUNWAY

So what do these aviation references have to do with the reinvention of your career or job? They represent the essential components for establishing your time and money runway for reinventing.

When Christofer reinvented his life from a classical musician to working in corporate finance, it took eighteen months of serious sacrifice, hard work and tenacity before he received his first paycheck. He sold everything, left his home, his family, even his poor dog, and moved into a small one-bedroom apartment. He had (what he thought was) enough cash to pay for tuition and living expenses for eighteen months. Eighteen months was the amount of time he thought it would take to finish his education and get a job.

In aviation terms, he drafted a flight plan (destination: new career), got rid of everything that was not essential (lightened his payload), and saved enough cash (fuel) to make the journey.

PAYLOAD ADJUSTMENT

Having a heavy payload (unsupportable lifestyle, habits/patterns of excessive spending) and little to no financial reserves is akin to attempting to take off with only a couple of gallons of fuel and packed to the hilt. Unless you're willing to make drastic lifestyle changes, you shouldn't even consider reinvention. If, however, you are truly interested in and are willing to make the necessary changes, now it's time to design your plan.

Before Damion's reinvention in 2006, he took a deep look into his burn rate (what he was spending on his day-to-day life). The surprise was when he compiled all the number and found was his AMEX burn rate was over $75,000 a month. Talk about a heavy payload ready to crash immediately after takeoff! There was no way to create a long enough runway with this type of weight. He was operating at full throttle, burning fuel like crazy though needing to slow down and conserve his fuel. Having a burn rate of almost a million a year meant being out of cash in a less than a year while attempting a reinvention from real estate to anything at all.

Before the reinvention started, he cut back on virtually everything of consequence. He severed the high-priced mentors, got rid of the castle on the golf course in exchange for an apartment, dumped the Ferrari in exchange for an eco-friendly cruiser, and eviscerated the ego spending. He managed to slash spending by over 90%, helped along by going into a near cash-only spending practice.

Something powerful happens when you have to use greenbacks to pay for everything. The spending becomes very real, and you become very conscious about your decisions, patterns and values.

When he switched into a hard cash mode, he thought twice about spending a few hundred dollars on a dinner, where in the past that would have been a non-event and an easy swipe of the AMEX Black card. He started shunning the doodads, clothes and other unnecessary junk that wasn't needed but wanted, a former drug of choice to stimulate the glands of excitement and satisfaction.

After having slashed his spending using a scorched earth policy, what remained was less than ten percent of the previous outflow. All of a sudden the runway to reinvention was clear for takeoff and the skies wide open for the period of time needed. He had enough fuel for two or three years to recreate and reinvent his mind.

Bottom line: Because of the sacrifices made in limiting his current lifestyle, he opened the door to creating a life far beyond anything he currently had.

THE CONVENIENT CHANGE OF PLAN

Plans are only good intentions unless they immediately degenerate into hard work.

—Peter Drucker

The building and execution of your reinvention plan is a very challenging process. It requires a good deal of tenacity and a Herculean amount of resolve, discipline and sacrifice to see it through to completion.

We end up where we are (good or bad) as a result of actions and habits that are usually driven by a considerable amount of unconscious behavior. There will be an unquantifiable parade of self-sabotaging opportunities and rationalizations to derail your plan, and they will all succeed until you become completely disgusted with your lack of progress and come to the realization that there is absolutely no choice but to follow through and stay the course. Something must become intolerable for you to make the changes, the sacrifices and the shift in direction to change your momentum.

You don't have to let go of every bad habit to make your reinvention work, just the most damaging ones, which if not discarded will impede all progress.

INEXCUSABLE EXCUSES

He that is good for making excuses is seldom good for anything else.

—Benjamin Franklin

Before we go delve into setting up your process, here are a few of my favorite excuses (for not sticking with the plan) from people who "*really decided to reinvent their lives*" before they fell off of the wagon.

1. Alan's plan included losing fifty pounds in a period of four months through a combination of dietary changes and practicing Tae Kwon Do. After three weeks of being on schedule, he mysteriously found himself at a Dairy Queen devouring his second Jumbo Turtle Waffle Bowl. "I had a bad day," was the excuse. "*I swear this will be my last Waffle Bowl until I lose the weight.*"

2. Renee's plan was to cease all new jewelry purchases yet
    somehow the David Yurman Rose Quartz Renaissance
    Bracelet (which, though discontinued from the collection
    three years ago, was brought back for a limited time and
    will "never be available again") ended up on her charge
    card and wrist. *"It is the missing piece in my David Yurman
    collection, and from this point on I am not purchasing any
    more jewelry,"* was the justification.

3. Dorothy's plan called for stopping all trips until she
    was generating enough income in her new profession to
    cover all living expenses. In an exquisite rationalization

and realization of self-sabotage, she raided $16,000 from her 401K to pay for a ten-day Christmas cruise on the Queen Mary 2, because *"life is short, and I will embrace austerity once back from Barbados."* The cruise deprived her of almost eight months of living expense and completely derailed her plan.

OUR RUNWAYS

He is the best man who, when making his plans, fears and reflects on everything that can happen to him, but in the moment of action is bold.

—Herodotus

Neither one of us had a mentor, role model or advisor who had successfully created something similar to our planned reinventions. Choosing the best course of action required a considerable amount of thought, research and planning.

CHRISTOFER'S STORY

I was absolutely certain that to effectively execute any plan, it was imperative that I remove several geographical references and habits tied to my old life. In other words, I had to completely disengage from my comfort zone and move.

On the tactical front, I'd taken a variety of business management, accounting and law courses without the intention of acquiring yet another degree. A number of the companies I interviewed with required employees to have a Master's degree in Business Administration (MBA) so I decided that part of my reinvention plan would include earning an MBA.

I recall going to the USC library to research MBA programs and was surprised to discover that there were over one hundred universities offering them. My plan was to be in school within one year and, not wanting to waste any time, defined the following criteria for choosing the schools to which I would apply:

- The curriculum had to be taught in either English or Spanish
- The school should be outside of the United States
- The course could be no longer than eighteen months
- There had to be a documented history of its MBA graduates being employed by well known organizations
- The total tuition could not cost more than $30,000.

Based on my available cash both from loans and reserves, my housing and incidentals budget couldn't exceed $2,000 per month or $36,000 over the planned eighteen months of study. In summary, this stage of my reinvention had to:

- Complete in eighteen months
- Not exceed a total budget of $66,000

After three months of research and sending out applications, I was accepted into an MBA program in the United Kingdom and within six months had packed my bags and moved.

OPTIONS AND THE BLACK SWAN EVENT

Creativity comes from looking for the unexpected and stepping outside your own experience

—Masaru Ibuka

Plans change regardless of one's steadfast commitment to staying the course. The best made plans can be altered by random and unexpected events that are beyond the normal expectations in any aspect of one's plans. These "Black Swan" events are simply beyond one's control and often beyond the mind to envision the remote possibility of their occurrence.

In my experience, due to the speed and timing of a Black Swan event, you don't have any time to react. The abject randomness of such events can be a superb opportunity to test one's survival skills and obtain an honest understanding of your true tenacity, intelligence and creativity.

As previously mentioned, I had a very tight budget and little or no room for error. The cost of living in the United Kingdom was materially more than had been anticipated, although I still had adequate cash reserves to get to the end of the eighteen-month runway. Then the Black Swan landed.

A massive currency devaluation of the United States Dollar vs. the British Pound hit, and my runway became a heliport. I found myself with only enough cash to fund four months of living expenses.

Being a full time student in a strenuous academic program didn't allow for any time to get a job (especially in a country that requires a work permit for non-citizens) so this was clearly not an option. I had to find $14,000 in ninety days or things were going to get very ugly. For a nanosecond I thought about trying to arrange a few recitals in the U.K. or Europe, event though the thought of going back to the world of classical guitar was a complete non-starter.

As part of the curriculum at the university, I attended a class on option trading—my least favorite lecture due to the monotone delivery by the corpse behind the lectern. When not enjoying a deep state of REM sleep, I did learn that in option trading it was possible to get enormous leverage and control a stock (for a limited period of time) without having to pay the market price for said stock. Since I didn't see any immediate options (no pun intended) to shore up my shortened runway, I decided to give option trading a try.

After losing about $3,000 in unfocused trading, I discovered a strategy called a *long straddle* (simultaneous purchase of an "at the money" call and a put option) and bought options on three companies namely The Mirror Group, News Corporation and Amstrad. To make a long story short, The Mirror Group's shares dropped by about eighty percent and News Corporation's shares went up by about twenty-five percent, which translated to my netting around $35,000. In my arrogance, I purchased another $10,000 of long straddles on the same equities and lost it all. Regardless of my loss, I was still up $25,000 overall, had replenished my cash reserves, and thus ended my short-lived career as an option trader.

LESSONS LEARNED

The best way to start mapping out your reinvention plans is to envision the end and start there. Take a piece of paper and (in as much detail as possible) describe how your reinvented life/career looks when complete. If there are some things that when acquired will complete a certain part of your plan, get pictures of them and keep them in a place where they're visible every day.

The next step is, working from the "end in mind," backfill the various steps in your plan until you arrive at the place where you are now. If you are nowhere now, that is fine as long as you have an idea where you're going.

This is not a New Age experiment but a powerful tool that has been most helpful in getting me through some challenging times. When I started my reinvention, I had a photo of a fifty-six-foot Hatteras and a Lear 25 in my journal. They were my constant companions through some bleak times. When I finally had the opportunity to experience them (if it floats or flies, always better to lease), the actual experiences were not as powerful as the images that pulled me through the difficult times.

DAMION'S STORY

The process of getting clear on my runway before diving head first into my reinvention was the key piece allowing me the time and space to find the truth and go all the way through the process. I knew I'd need a couple years to heal, adjust and dig into the deepest levels of what I was searching for. Knowing my reinvention was going to be a multi-year process and being rational about my spending needs, not wants, I had the insight about how long my resources would last.

Only after I'd cut away all the unnecessary stuff, junk and clutter, and stopped the excess consumption habits did I have the ability to enter the chamber of reinvention. I can't even begin to stress how important it is minimize your "needs" if you really want to reinvent. If you insist on living the status quo with all the accouterments you're used to, you are basically dead in the water in terms of having any type of runway that won't result in a crash landing and a giant fireball.

The truth is that most things we think we need are really wants in disguise. Most wants are really temporary band-aids to patch up and cover our exposed insecurities we'd rather ignore and not face.

QUESTIONS & ACTIONS

1. Write your "what it looks like when it is done" description and select some powerful images to remind you of where you are going.
2. Assuming your planned reinvention will require that you leave your current place of employment, calculate how long can you survive on your total cash savings.
3. For thirty days, track and list all of your expenses, dividing them into fixed costs (those items that are the same every month—*e.g.*, rent, car payments, insurance, etc.) and variable costs (eating out, groceries, clothes, gifts).
4. Figure out and write out the needed elements and processes for your reinvention. List them and write down how long they will take to achieve and their costs. Once you have this timeline and using your current monthly expenditures, calculate how much money you will need to get to the finish line. For example, if it costs you $3,000 (combined fixed and variable costs) per month to live and you need to go back to school for one year, you will need approximately $36,000 of runway to fund

your reinvention assuming there is no change in your lifestyle.

5. If you have enough capital to fund everything, then by all means continue with the Dairy Queen and Neiman Marcus spending. If not, take the list from Item 3 and decide what can be cut. You have to be brutally honest: Ask what you need to survive, not to be comfortable. Your ability to identify and eliminate nonessential expenditures is a good indicator of your ability and level of commitment to the reinvention of your life. If you don't want to change your current habits, then don't even bother contemplating a reinvention.

6. Take all of the elements from the previous four exercises, put them into a binder, and find someone (no relatives or partners) with financial expertise with whom you can discuss your plan. Be candid with them about your plan and do NOT argue. Listen and take notes.

7. Stay away from the Jumbo Turtle Waffle Bowls.

8
METRICS

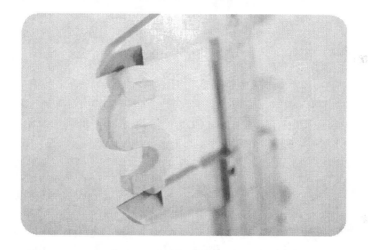

def.

A set of measurements that quantify results. Performance metrics quantify the unit's performance. Project metrics tell you whether the project is meeting its goals. Business metrics define the business's progress in measurable terms.

> *If it can be measured, it can be managed.*
> —Old Business Adage

On Making Assumptions...

The power of generalizing and making assumptions gives men considerable superiority in making mistakes as compared with dumb animals.

—George Eliot

AN OVERVIEW

M etrics for your Reinvented Life have to do with the statistical and quantifiable numbers in a given profession as they relate to the average income, requirements of generating income, probability of achieving a consistent level of income, and time required to achieve a desired level of consistent income.

There is a common perception/misperception that attempting to quantify the financial attributes of a profession or project will somehow drive the spirit/fun/excitement out of it. "Do what you love and the money will follow," "the sky's the limit," and "be the best you can be and you will be provided with all that you need," are just a few of the well worn quotes from the financial lexicon of urban legend. Though emotionally satisfying, the aforementioned clichés are generally not allies in your goal to understand the financial metrics of your career/job reinvention.

Perhaps you're considering the reinvention of your life due to a serious level of dissatisfaction with your current career, or maybe you lost your job and now need to completely re-educate yourself to find employment. Wherever you're at in the process of your reinvention, the best and only time to start is now.

The majority of all professions, jobs and businesses have their own set of metrics. These metrics aren't difficult to discover with a little work. As better questions will usually beget better answers, I suggest asking yourself (and write this down!) the following questions regarding your current or contemplated reinvention.

1. Why I am doing this?
2. If I decide not to pursue a reinvention, what will my life look like in one, three or five years?
3. What skills/education/time commitment is required?
4. How much can I realistically make at the inception as well as the peak of my earning power in this new job/career/profession?
5. Are my financial expectations and needs realistic? And (without a miracle occurring) can they be realized in this new job/career/profession?
6. Am I willing to pay the price (assuming you understand the price) to do this?

Intelligent and thoughtful answers to these questions are an efficient manner to start the process of your discovery.

CHRISTOFER'S STORY

But little Mouse, you are not alone
In proving foresight may be vain:
The best laid schemes of mice and men
Go often awry,
And leave us nothing but grief and pain,
For promised joy!
—Robert Burns

I studied and trained to be a classical guitarist from the age of seven. I must have been reasonably talented as the studies evolved into an interesting (though not financially lucrative) profession that gave me the opportunity to teach, record and perform beautiful music on both the national and international level.

I never thought about the financial aspects of the profession until I reached my late teens because the majority of my time was consumed in practice, master classes and academic studies. If invited to perform a solo recital or with an ensemble, a ticket would be purchased for me and all other accommodations (food and lodging) were always provided.

I was not accustomed to thinking about the future, and when any thought of money came to mind, there was an unspoken and absurd assumption that I was going to be rich, famous, and have the career of a touring virtuoso. There had been enough "confirmation events" to make me believe my own erroneous story as by twenty-two years of age, I had flown in a private jet, made a record at Abbey Road Studios (where my heroes

The Beatles had worked), and performed recitals in Vienna, London, Geneva and Paris (to name a few).

So what does this have to do with discovering the metrics of a reinvented career or profession? Have patience—the intent here is to demonstrate what happens when one starts to ask different questions and the resulting answers and perceptions start to appear in your life. Other parts of this book elaborate on "trigger events" and their effect in initiating change in one's life. The first major one for me—which eventually led to the entire reinvention of my life and profession—was in Paris, France, and unfolded as follows:

AN AWAKENING IN PARIS

I was invited to perform in a chamber music festival being held at the magnificent San Chapelle on Île de la Cité in the heart of Paris. My repertoire for the evening consisted of a concerto by Antonio Vivaldi, a quintet by Luigi Boccherini and a transcription of a Lute Suite by Weiss. The recital was a success and the audience provided a standing ovation, a few bouquets of flowers, and asked for an encore.

After the concert, accompanied by two members of the group, I took a walk and ended up in front of the Hotel George V. Feeling rather full of myself, I invited my guests for a drink and then decided to check into the hotel as a reward for such a great performance. My first shock was when I paid for the drinks, but the real surprise came when I realized the price of a room for one night was three times the fee I had received for my concert performance.

It was the first time in my life that *I felt poor* and began giving thought to the financial limitations of my chosen profession. Rather than creating despondency, this experience and the associated feelings pushed me to begin a research project to discover the financial metrics of my chosen profession.

THE PROCESS BEGINS–RESEARCH

Research is what I'm doing when I don't know what I'm doing.

—Werner von Braun

On the flight back to my home in the United States, I wrote down all of the areas in which a classical guitarist could create income, which were:

1. Performing concerts
2. Teaching master classes or private students
3. Making records
4. Teaching at a university

I decided that the first step in discovering the financial metrics of being a classical performer would be to start with obtaining the concert fees of the players who were at the top of the profession. The universe of performers was small, but obtaining the information was extremely difficult.

The second part of my research was to create a short- and long-term wish list (and associated costs) of a number of things that I wanted to have in the next two years (new car, new guitar and purchase of an apartment). I also made a list of a number of things that I wanted to own or experience when I "made my fortune" as a classical musician. Amongst the magnanimous desires of solving world hunger and spending time with the Dali Lama, the long-term list included a home in the Barrio Santa Cruz in Seville, Spain; a beach property in the Grenadines; a home in Laguna Beach, California; a Bentley Turbo R; and the ability (whenever I desired) to travel and stay at the Peninsula Hotel in New York, the Hotel George V in Paris, or the Lanesborough in London.

Of the many things I discovered in my research, the most disturbing was the realization that the majority of my assumptions regarding the income metrics of my chosen profession were completely wrong and based on hope rather than facts. If the very best performers in the industry (based on the information I was able to obtain) would more than likely not be able to afford the lifestyle and things I had on my wish list, then the probability that I could achieve my financial dreams in this profession were somewhere in a probability range of low to impossible. The other fact I discovered was that if I really looked at the income I was making at the current time, my ability to acquire even the "humble" items on the first of my two lists was going to be equally challenging.

I enjoyed playing music, but I wanted an affluent lifestyle. And the two were in *direct conflict with each other.*

LESSONS LEARNED

> *You must stick to your convictions, but be prepared to abandon your assumptions.*
> —Denis Waitley

It is very easy to believe one's own stories (whether or not they are true), especially if there is no one in your life who, without assassinating your character and dreams, has the experience and willingness to provide reasonable and factual guidance. The majority of people's direct and consistent relationships are either through default (work in the same office, belong to the same club) or familial. If one is fortunate enough to have someone in your immediate social or familial circle who has the experience, expertise and willingness to assist in answering the difficult and important questions as they pertain to your career or job goals, you are the exception to the rule.

It is generally not human nature to seek people who challenge or critique our dreams and goals as such things (until given the opportunity to be proven) are usually fragile in their composition. The people who *"support us for whoever we are,"* or tell us that *"you can have whatever you want if you really put your mind to it,"* generally do not have the domain specific skills or abilities to add value in such a critical area as the reinvention of your job or career.

These people can be reassuring as a personification of love and loyalty in your life, though if you really want loyalty and unconditional acceptance, get a dog. If you're serious about your reinvention, avoid the canine cheerleaders and seek the hard facts.

SUMMARY

Whenever you want to achieve something, keep your eyes open, concentrate and make sure you know exactly what it is you want. No one can hit their target with their eyes closed.

—Paulo Coelho, *The Devil and Miss Prym*

It's very easy to get confused and led astray by the plethora of self-help methodologies that seem to always hover around the periphery of our lives. Walk into any bookstore (especially at an airport) and you'll see dozens of books telling you how the author(s) lost weight, made a billion dollars, met their soul mate, found their spiritual guide, and took a ride in a UFO. With the exception of the UFO experience, you might learn something from buying one of these books, but it will never be a substitute for taking the necessary tactical steps reinvent *your life.*

Time is the one thing that we cannot get back once it is used. I would venture that since you are reading these words and want a reinvention of your life, you want to get down to business and not waste any time.

My process of discovery was entirely self-directed out of necessity as there was no one in my life who had a clue about the financial metrics of my profession or had experienced the material things and experiences that were part of my wish lists. But when I began to ask the right questions, the honest answers started to appear.

QUESTIONS & ACTIONS

Consider the following items/suggestions in beginning the process of your reinvention:

1. Seek the counsel of people who have, more or less, done what you are planning to do. If they are not in your immediate social or familial circle, then use a social network or any other means necessary to locate them.

2. Develop a set of intelligent questions and don't beat around the bush. If you want to change your profession from machinist to Yoga instructor, find two or three people who are supporting themselves as yoga instructors. Ask about their hours worked on a weekly and monthly basis, the training they received, costs of training, employment opportunities, benefits for employees, how much money

they make (they might even tell you), and how long it took them to get to that level of income.

3. Don't look for the answers that make you feel good; look for the answers that fit your questions. If the person(s) with whom you are speaking cannot provide answers to all of your questions, then find someone else who can until the entire list of questions is answered to your satisfaction.

4. You are making a huge change so spend time getting very clear on what your new life/career/job is going to look like as it relates to time commitment, personal income, changes in the way you currently live, and relationships (personal and professional).

5. Write an operating budget (all of your expenses) and evaluate its relationship to the potential and immediate (if available) income in your new reinvented job/career. If you need $3,000 per month to pay your bills and the new career/position will pay nothing for six months, then you need $18,000 in cash or credit reserves to make the change. You will need a long enough runway to pull this off so make sure that you have planned accordingly. Whatever you do, avoid delegating this exercise to the "*I just know things will work out and don't want to focus on money*" mindset. Things might work out, but it's always better to plan for the worse and hope for the best.

6. Understand the basis for your reinvention. If the motivation is about creating a better income, then be clear (based on the information you have gathered in your research) that there is a higher than average probability that you will be able to create a better income. Understand what it will take from your life (the price you will pay) in order to achieve this. If the

motivation is driven by the need for a different lifestyle, try experiencing the desired lifestyle to see if it suits you. Once you check out of your past, it becomes difficult or impossible to check back in.

7. If the basis for your reinvention is to have a better car, a bigger house, to live near the beach, and/or spend more time in meditation, try renting or living the experience on a short-term basis before rearranging your life based on an unknown set of facts and experiences. (I have a friend who quit his job, sold his house, and moved to the Caribbean as it had been his lifelong dream to escape the miserable weather in northern England. After spending eight months in "paradise," he decided that it was not for him and returned to England, where he experienced considerable emotional and financial hardship when trying to recreate his old lifestyle. He later told me that he wished that he had taken the time to actually visit the location of his dreams before making such a radical decision.—Christofer)

8. Once you have enough facts to make a decision about the best course of action for your reinvented life/career, write out a plan (as if you were doing it for someone else) of the steps that must be taken to begin the process. If you don't know how to do this, find someone who can help you. You might be surprised who will show up.

9. Don't get bogged down with writing mission statements, making vision boards, or constructing business plans. That can come later or perhaps there will never be a need for it. Now is the time to begin the step-by-step execution of your plan.

10. Find someone to whom you can be accountable to make sure you are making progress and moving toward the

vision and financial metrics of your reinvented life. Avoid individuals (unless they have gone through this process and were successful) who will soften the truth or conversely not give you praise and guidance for your progress. This is called tactical alchemy. To get more on this go to www.ReinventedLife.com and type: ACCOUNTABILITY.

9

ACTION-CORRECTION CYCLE

def.

action

> *The fact or process of doing something, typically to achieve an aim: "demanding tougher action against terrorism."*

correction

> *A change that rectifies an error or inaccuracy.*

cycle

A series of events that are regularly repeated in the same order.

If you want to succeed, double your failure rate.
—Thomas J. Watson

THEORY

We are meant to be in motion. As human beings we are not meant to be idle without movement in life. Without movement, we atrophy and die. In movement we learn, grow and improve. The challenge is that we don't have an operating manual so much of what we do is a guess. Think about being a parent,: You do the best you can and hopefully you learn, correct and do better the next time. Think about investing: You take action, screw things up, lose money, learn, correct and do something different or better the next time. This cycle of constant action and correction is the basis of growth and the key to fulfillment.

The theory is easy—until you start or think about starting. Then you freeze.

But why? Often you run square into one of the saboteurs below. Only action can break the ritual and the habits of the saboteurs. Taking action breaks the habit, changes your state, and gives you a chance to correct and grow out of the circular cycle you're stuck in.

Common archetype saboteurs that keep you stuck and that you'll continue fighting are:

- **The Child**: You are entirely naïve and innocent. You focus on family and fun.
- **The Victim**: You blame others for your situation. Nothing is your fault, and taking responsibility is a foreign idea.
- **The Drama Queen**: You feed on drama—the more, the better.
- **The Prostitute**: You're willing to sell your soul, your integrity, more morals, your anything. You are for sale.

And from Aristotle, we learn these three traps common to all humanity:

- **Learned Helplessness**: You accept as fact a certain limiting belief—and since it's always been that way, it always will be that way. You accept it as is.
- **Comfort Zone**: You are trapped by your fear of the unknown. Since self-improvement is the result of change, everything you want by definition lies outside your comfort zone. If you refuse to be unconformable, you are rejecting any possibility of improvement.
- **Path of Least Resistance**: You go for the easiest, fastest route instead of being willing to put the time and energy into anything that could truly improve your life. Mastery often requires years. There's no "secret" or short cut or golden goose. But fear or boredom (which is often fear in disguise) keeps you from making the effort.

EDUCATION SYSTEM—CLASS IDIOT BILLIONAIRE

The education system is set up to reward perfection and to condemn mistakes. Mistakes are called failing, and the person who makes the most mistakes is the class idiot. In the real world the person who makes the most mistakes is called Thomas Edison, Abraham Lincoln or the next dot-com millionaire. In reality the only way you learn is to take action and then learn from what you've done so you can adjust and continue in motion. Buckminster Fuller said, "Humans are meant to be in motion," and by that he meant you are purposefully given a body to use, move and trigger things. You are not meant to live in your mind alone.

The idea that you can think your way to happiness, think your way to wellness, think your way to wealth, or think your way to anything else is pure madness. The notion that by some law of attraction you can think your way into having a bag of money drop from the sky and hit you in the head is about the stupidest thing we've been sold on.

LAW OF AWARENESS

The law of attraction would be relevant with the twist that it was called the law of awareness. When you're aware, also known as conscious, you suddenly see things that were right in front of you all along. Have you ever all of a sudden noticed how many other people drive the same type of car you just bought? It happens to everybody. You don't notice something that's been there all along until you were suddenly conscious of it. You are only aware of what you choose to focus on.

The action-correction cycle requires awareness + action. Just because you're aware that you are broke and want to be rich (or fat and want to become fit, etc.) doesn't mean it will happen simply by thinking about it a lot. Your body must take action. In your mind you've taken action so the external form of that is the next natural step. But wait, why doesn't it happen naturally and automatically?

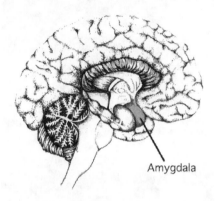

Amygdala

PAIN

The fear of pain prevents the action. You've either had an experience of pain in a previous action or you've heard a story (or made up a story in your mind) about how that action causes pain. In either case your mind triggers the amygdala to keep us safe, and as a result, you freeze, in an effort to guarantee survival. Much like your amygdala will instinctually keep you from walking towards a bear, it will also do whatever it can to steer you away from the potential of pain. It's doing its job to protect you from dying, but it is acting on a very primitive level that is counterproductive to the modern human. The amygdala simply hasn't evolved as fast as your consciousness and human potential has. The amygdala is still in the Neanderthal era, worried about you being eaten by saber-toothed tigers.

To get past the Amygdala, it's usually easier to take some small action that doesn't risk the hazard of death. Tightrope walkers usually train with a net until they're confident enough to out their lives on the line (literally), and you probably want to learn to play an instrument before you quit your job to become a rock star. Your amygdala rightly lashes back at those types of moves in an attempt to protect you from yourself.

Once you take some action, assuming it doesn't kill you, you'll get feedback and your job is to learn. What happened? What worked, what didn't, what can I use from this to get better? The next step is to take more action, learn more, and keep correcting.

The secret to this process is not that you can take action, which most people do every day when they get out of bed and take a shower. The secret is to develop the rituals and habits that will constantly give you feedback and then using that feedback to learn and correct. The two ways to learn and correct we've found most useful are: 1) journaling with think time and 2) accountability partners.

Journaling with think time, as already mentioned, is key during this process so the jumbled thoughts in your head and the invaluable lessons from your mistakes can be learned from and not repeated

When you ask a question and then start writing the answer, you'll find your mind provides amazing insights and fear starts to vanish. Asking a question like, "How can I create an extra $500 per month in income?" or "What one thing could I do that would make my customers such raving fans that they'd never even consider going to the competition?" and then writing down whatever your mind comes up with can be an astonishingly illuminating experience. You'll get tons of answers, including LOTS of bad ones! The point is to get them out.

Next, pick something on your list and do it, start it, get going! Then ask the question, "What worked with this, did I give it enough time, can I tweak it with what I've learned or should I throw it away and try another course of action?" Once you have the answer, get your body in motion again! Tweak your last thing or try something altogether new—either way, just so long as you learn from it. Most of what you do will not work, but that's the point! We're learning beings, not perfectly infallible machines.

ACCOUNTABILITY PARTNERS

Accountability partners act in the same way and can be used throughout the process. In the beginning you have an idea or perhaps you have a trigger event and something snaps. Grab your partner and discuss your ideas. Then commit your first steps—specific measurable steps with definite deadlines. Go do it, and then come back to your partner and discuss. Invite your partner to give you honest, candid feedback and course correct based on what you've learned.

Never take this feedback personally. Your job is to listen. Understand that one of the greatest gifts you can ever receive is the honest, candid feedback from someone else on your life. The reason it's such a gift is because your accountability partner is shedding light on your *blind spots* that you have absolutely no chance of seeing. No matter how hard you think or look out in front of you, you have blind spots behind you that you can't see—but the person looking at you can see with crystal clarity. The more feedback you get, the more course corrections you can make. And as you make corrections, the more distinctions you'll be able to make and the finer those distinctions will be... leading you towards mastery, the ultimate goal.

Distinctions make all the difference in your drive towards mastery. For example, Damion grew up in Alaska while Christofer grew up in the sun. How many words did the Eskimos in Alaska have for snow? Between thirty and three hundred. How many did Christofer have? Probably one. Why the difference? Because having finer distinctions for that word was important for life and for survival. There was not much need to describe snow thirty different ways in the Caribbean, but the subtle differences in Alaska to an Eskimo can mean the difference between life and death.

The more you course correct, the more words you'll have for snow, and the more distinctions you'll develop.

Keys:

- STOP talking! Listen ninety percent of the time. We learn by listening. And when you are talking, focus on contribution, not self-aggrandizement.
- Speed kills/Patience pays. Everyone wants to make a quick buck (or a quick million) without doing much work and they want it today. But anything you gain in a reckless fashion will be lost just as quickly, because that's the way your mind is operating. Pursuing your goals with full awareness may take longer, but the results will be stable and lasting.
- Focus on the means, not the result. Fall in love with the cause, and let the effect take care of itself. Keep correcting until you get the positive taps of confirmation that you're on the right path.

DAMION'S STORY

MONEY

For the couple years I spent hiding from the truth and from everything and everybody, I was going through the motions, doing just enough to get by, and I felt like a total waste of space. I'd go out to eat, go on a date, have some drinks, dip my toes in a venture here or there, lose money in it, and make no progress in any direction.

In the course of reinventing my financial life after the economic meltdown in 2008, I asked a friend of mine who also had experienced some disruption in his life with the downturn to join me in an accountability partnership. We met every three months in person and spoke every couple weeks. We discussed what we were doing and what we were struggling with and gave the other feedback. My friend—we'll call him Cliff—saw me bouncing around from idea to idea, trying countless random things, and frittering away my time and energy, And he would ask me why I was doing them and how they were contributing to my goals.

In the beginning of the partnership, I would sometimes push back and try to validate my decisions without embracing his feedback. I was still hiding in my lies, to myself, and dwelling on the First Order consequences, *i.e.*, doing what felt good.

As time went on and my life seemed to continue on in status quo (the status quo being generally shitty), I finally started implementing the course corrections he recommended. And suddenly I started getting different results. I paid attention to those results, documented what I'd done, and embraced what became of it.

TRACKING

I tracked my spending for two straight years, writing down every penny I personally spent. I watched in horror as I was unconsciously and habitually spending $100-$200 a month on coffee, $1,000 a month going out to eat, and thousands of dollars a month on shiny fun stuff that seemed fun in principle but only collected dust in reality. I course corrected as this came to light. In real time I adjusted my habits. I didn't cut everything off; I simply got conscious and made some different choices—some simple, some profound. I decided to go to Starbucks on the weekends and to make coffee at home during the week. I used cash only to buy anything other than groceries.

VISCERAL SPENDING

By the way, using cash is a powerful way to slow out-of-control spending. There's something far more real and visceral with cash when you physically hand it over to another person. Swiping a piece of plastic is a huge disconnect and easier to lose control with. When I bought my Ferrari, I have no doubt I would have never bought it if I had personally hand over $2,500 in cash each and every month. I might as well have been throwing it in my fireplace. To me that was the same effect as owning the Ferrari, because that's what it cost just to have the thing in my garage every month, before I even took it out.

The more visceral, the more leverage I got on the course correction cycle.

I remember when I became conscious of alcohol and realized how much I was drinking. I nearly threw up when I started calculating the volume. I tracked the number of drinks I had each day, and after a year I remember saying to Cliff, "Man, do you realize this is like 200 bottles of wine?" I thought about the liver trauma, the poor decisions I'd made with the alcohol, and the amount of money I spent on it. I did what is called "stacking." I stacked all these negatives on top of each other, and practically overnight the volume of alcohol shriveled to a minimum.

If something starts nipping at me and I sense it's a problem, now I ask the question, "What are the facts? What's really happening, what are the numbers?" I track it and then decide whether the numbers are supporting me or distracting me from my higher order needs. The level of consciousness in this activity will take your breath away.

WELLNESS

An enormous problem in society, especially in the United States, is the explosion of obesity. We are constantly unconsciously consuming junk, and with largely lethargic lifestyles we're getting fatter and fatter. I was no exception, and pre-reinvention I crossed over the two hundred pound, multi-layered-chin, man-boob threshold. I had absolutely no idea the slope I was sliding down until one day I had a trigger event—a mini wellness trigger event—when my friend Rich emailed me a photo of him before and after losing one hundred pounds in the previous six months. I was shocked—and then I was even more shocked when I looked in the mirror and, in horror, realized I was turning into a whale, one quad caramel Frappuccino and pasta Alfredo dish at a time.

The course correction happened instantly. I asked what he did, and I used it as a model. That night I signed up for the e-course he'd used called the Adonis System and joined the support community. I set off on December 5th to correct the unconscious disaster I'd created with my body. By April 5th I was fit, trim and down more than forty pounds from my heaviest. The key? I got conscious and recognized what is. Specifically, I recognized, "I is fat!" Now, what do I need to do to not be fat?

I need to eat less and work out more. Okay, so how? I quantified that by figuring out what my BMI was and the number of calories I'd been eating by default. I made sure to eat less than that, and I worked out six days a week with weights according to the Adonis System. Every day I wrote down what I ate, the number of calories consumed, and what I'd burned doing the workouts. Within weeks it was clear and obvious what had happened. My unconscious habits of having an Amy's pizza at 10 or 11 p.m., a few beers, snacks during the day, bread (oooh baby, bread is death), and on and on, had added up to me being a fatty.

Pre-reinvention, the feedback I'd received from people was always loving and kind, "Oh, D, you look great!" My girlfriends never said, "Dude, go to the gym!" That supportive feedback only supported me turning into a cow. Nobody was telling me the truth, not even me, especially not me!

It's been years since that snap, and the action correction cycle continues. I constantly look in the mirror, ask myself how I'm feeling, write down how many calories I'm consuming, and acknowledge when I'm feeling sexy or feeling like Jabba the Hutt. The constant question, "What is true?" keeps me conscious and in integrity with my wellness.

RELATIONSHIPS

Before the trigger event, in the years leading up to the reinvention, I had a series of relationships that although outwardly different were effectively the same over and over again in a variety of forms and hairstyles.

I met someone, wooed her, captured her, and got bored with her. I'd get frustrated with her lack of ambition, lack of intelligence, lack of common sense, lack of physical beauty, lack of something, and I'd go into an inverted action-correction cycle. My form of correction in these relationships was to become such a jerk that the women would get frustrated and leave. They'd finally give up because they couldn't figure me out. If they held on, this was my indicator that I needed to take stronger action—specifically, I needed to be a bigger jerk—and that would get the job done. If that didn't work, I'd correct into supreme asshole until the outcome was achieved.

If that still didn't work, I'd start a relationship with someone else in an attempt to show the original person I wasn't interested and had moved on. This was my mechanism to get the job done because I had neither the balls nor the integrity to walk away and call it off. Yes, it's embarrassing, and yes, I was a schmuck. I was scared of being exposed, and I was scared of anyone getting close. This cycle helped make sure the few amazing relationships and women I shared time with were sacrificed so I could learn and go through the process.

The regret isn't so much that I'm not with them today because needed to learn the lesson. The regret is pain I inflicted on these gentle souls.

COURSE CORRECTION

After the reinvention I decided I needed to dig into my soul in order to figure out what the heck was going on and to design my perfect vision for a relationship. I was convinced that if I could just get clear on what she looked like, what she did, how she acted, her pedigree, etc., then all my problems would be solved and Ms. Spectacular would arrive.

Nice try. After about six months of conversations with my therapist, dating a number of different women, having one relationship blow up like the old ones did, and feeling like I still wasn't really finding the perfect woman, I suddenly realized I was seeking meaningful inside a lie. The mind I was in seeking answers was the manager/manipulator mind and could/would only ever be successful connecting with women in a shallow way, through management and manipulation.

After months of peeling back layer upon layer of my mind, going on endless dates, analyzing the dates, the actions, the thoughts, correcting and then doing it again, I finally realized I had to exchange minds and only after entering the mind of truth would I be able to share myself in a harmonious relationship. But I had to be willing to share the space from an honest mind, not a mind of lies.

TWO MINDS

I learned that we have both minds and we can operate from either of them at any time. You might call this the dark side, your little devil, the "other version" of self. My lie/fear mind was the one that had all the power for years and focused on getting what it wanted to protect itself from being exposed to the world.

Once I learned how to tap into the honest mind, the mind of truth, I took action and went on a date at the lake. I remember having a conversation with this girl and sharing all my dark "stuff," a resume of my dating history and more. She looked at me in horror and squeaked something out about how that was a lot to share. I thought, "Great! This is the key! Just give them everything and it will work!" That was the last time I ever heard from her. Clearly vomiting on people is not so attractive.

Over the next year I learned the subtle distinction between knowing the truth and being able to delineate when it's appropriate to share or not share. The further I disempowered my lying mind and embraced my honest mind, the more I found I was okay sharing and I was okay not sharing.

I realized through asking the question, "Why am I sharing?" that the answer was often times to feed my ego and put myself on the "honesty king" box. I was proving how honest I could be, like Brad Blanton suggests in "Radical Honesty."

Finally, I found myself sharing when I had the invitation to share and sharing with appropriate discretion. I've made incredible mistakes costing millions of dollars and causing raging rivers of tears, but those mistakes can't be changed by dumping them on everyone I encounter. When appropriate I'm happy and open to share any part of my life. The cloak or veil of deceit is gone. I've also learned the answer isn't sticking a finger down my throat at first introduction. The answer isn't to avoid a tough or uncomfortable conversation. The answer is to be kind and honest and share space when another wishes to share.

CYCLES

MONEY

Create a financial statement. If you don't know how, get help. This one piece of reality will help your financial life as much as anything else you can do.

Track your spending patterns. Are you spending more than you make each month? This one's easy to figure out because either your debt is increasing each month or it's decreasing. If it's increasing, you're spending more than you make. STOP DOING THAT!

Once you're not spending more than you make, start spending less. How?

Take something right off the top and invest it somewhere you can't get to and that you'll never think about. Consider this investment a payment to yourself, and pay yourself first—even if it's $1 a week. Get in the habit and gradually increase it.

Get feedback from someone on what your blind spots are. Ask your accountability partner what he or she sees. Are you constantly going to Starbucks like I was, dropping $6 a day or $200 a month? Are you leasing an $800 Tahoe when you could be payment free with an Accord? What are you doing that you're not seeing?

CAREER

Ever heard of Go to Work with Your Parents Day? It's never too late to try Work Your Dream Job Day. Find someone doing what you think you'd like to do and ask them if you can volunteer for them. Tell them you'll do anything they want to help them out if you're allowed to see what their day looks like. Most people will be honored that you think so highly of them to want to see their "so cool" career. Now watch, take notes, and course correct your assumptions about what that world looks like.

Ask those who've already hit the top of their game if you can buy them a cup of coffee and spend twenty or thirty minutes asking them questions about how they got to where they are. Offer to pay them for their time. If they say yes, pay them. This is something I call a doofus test. I often tell someone I will be happy to meet with them for coffee and I charge $500 an hour. If they aren't willing to pay $250 to get a shortcut from my experiences and learn from me, then I'm probably wasting my time and they probably won't take what I recommend very seriously. If someone wants to meet you at 6:00 a.m. forty miles from where you live, go, listen, learn. Then correct your action plan.

RELATIONSHIPS

Who's your model? Do you have a model of a great relationship? Spend time with people who have great relationships and observe how they interact with each other. I remember watching how one of my friends Keith would interact with his wife Sandi and thinking, "Wow, now that's a world-class way to be in a relationship." I watched carefully how much respect they had for each other and how they made each other their mutual top priority. They exemplify the model of a spectacular relationship.

Get a neutral opinion: Go to a counselor with your partner or by yourself if you're alone, and ask, "What am I not seeing, how can I be better?" Then shut up, listen, take notes, and correct whatever you're messing up on.

Read *His Needs, Her Needs*, *The 5 Love Languages* and all of John Gray's stuff.

HEALTH

Get clear with where you are. Ask yourself what would be considered an improvement. Would losing ten pounds and keeping it off be progress? Focus on progress that sticks through habits. Do this: Keep track of what you're consuming by writing it down every day. Write down what you're doing activity-wise. See what your habits are over a month and start adjusting a little at a time. The results will arrive because the inputs are different. By the way if you smoke, STOP! This is hands-down the most important decision you'll ever make to improve your health. There's virtually nothing more devastating on the body than the damage from smoking.

QUESTIONS & ACTIONS

1. Who kicks your ass when you go off course? And how often does it get kicked?
2. Do you think that money can fix the majority of problems? Are you sure?
3. What is the consistent thing or behavior that sabotages your life and work?

10
BUCKY 5: OSMOTIC ADAPTION

def.

osmosis

1. The tendency of molecules of a solvent to pass through
    a semipermeable membrane from a less concentrated
    solution into a more concentrated one.

2. The process of gradual or unconscious assimilation of ideas, knowledge, etc.

adaption

The process of adapting to something (such as environmental conditions)

> *As the saying goes that a man is known by the company he keeps. Good company can make a man whereas bad company can ruin him.*
>
> —Sam Veda

> *You are the average of the five people you spend the most time with.*
>
> —Jim Rohn

THEORY

The five people you spend most of your time with will in large part determine what your life looks like, PERIOD. In fact, if you look around you right now at the five people you're spending most of your time with and take a broad-strokes average of them in every way (financially, physically, intellectually, emotionally, spiritually), you are likely an average of the five. We suggest you not argue with this but rather think about it and ask yourself, "If my character were to be assessed by the company I keep, would I be ostracized or embraced by those I wish to be in relationship with?"

When you're unsure of a man's character, look at his friends.

—David Ryder

The company you keep is a reflection of your values and who you are. The power to choose, as J. Martin Kohe says in *Your Greatest Power*, is the most amazing thing and it is innately human, the one thing that separates us from all other animals. However, as our friend the Grail Knight from *Indiana Jones and the Last Crusade* says, "You must choose. But choose wisely for as the true Grail will bring you life, the false Grail will take it from you." True friends and company will bring you life while the false friends will take it from you.

BLIND SPOTS

True friends tell us the truth. They will say what needs to be said. They care about us enough and the trust between us is strong enough that even when the words may hurt our feelings, they're honoring the relationship by sharing what they see, even (or especially) when we can't. They're giving us a view of our blind spots.

We refer the five people closest to you as your "Bucky 5" (after the great Buckminster Fuller). To be sure you're choosing them wisely, you have to ask yourself the right questions.

Who is telling you the TRUTH? Who is calling it right? Are you sure? The higher you go in your mission, your purpose, your destiny, the greater the requirement to have someone around you to tell you the truth. The only hurdle between here and where you want to be is the support of others.

DAMION'S STORY

Before my reinvention I bought many of my friendships by "loaning" my partners money to live, paying for almost everything for everyone around me when we socialized, and subconsciously maintaining myself as the smartest and richest guy in the room. At least, that was the image I worked to create. I remember going to China and buying knockoff Rolex watches with Park, one of my old partners. We proudly and presumptuously wore those watches around in an attempt to project how rich and successful we were to other people we didn't even know. Park was a reflection of me at the time: deceptive, self-centered and, in his case, actually evil.

I remember one day during the reinvention realizing that even my watches were lies. To be in harmony between my mind of truth and the projection of the truth, I threw them out at once. Since my internal compass of truth had gained so much power, anything I came into contact with that was non-true was rapidly dismissed or discarded. The things and people I'd engaged with in the previous time with my previous mind now made me nauseous to be near. My internal guide became highly sensitive to B.S. and it rejected it outright. My new mind would call itself to arms if anything other than truth tried to get close and invade.

THINKING TYPES

In the old mind, I focused on best-case scenarios almost exclusively, ignoring the realistic scenarios or worst-case scenarios. My optimistic thinking was fabulous, but my realistic thinking was lacking. A great resource for exploring these different types of thinking is John Maxwell's *Thinking for a Change*. The problem with only being optimistic is that it leads you to believe a train won't run you over and flatten you dead if you stand up on the train tracks as it barrels towards you at sixty miles an hour. Realistic thinking is crucial and every bit as important as optimistic thinking.

Pre-reinvention, I had a group of friends who were mostly going sideways, not really growing or becoming better in much of anything, and certainly not striving for mastery. They were happy with their lives or at least not unhappy enough to improve or change.

In the meantime, I spent most of my time learning, changing, growing and evolving, and still kept many of the same people around to feel good about the contrast. The accolades from the weak and the lazy felt good. I felt superior to many of them, and my game of King of the Hill was well played in my insecure mind.

A number of financially well-off people I spent time with were making lots of money through lies, deceit and coercion. Upon reflection, their techniques and virtues were perfectly in line with my previous mind, a nauseating recollection. I remember one of my girlfriends being publically acknowledged and admired by one of my mentors because she was making a million bucks a year as a mortgage broker. She worked only fifteen to twenty hours a week and seemed to have it all figured out. She did—she'd figured out how to make a lot of money by lying and cheating.

I'm actually surprised she didn't go to prison after the economic meltdown considering the number of stated income loans she did with fabricated supporting documentation. I remember her telling clients and other brokers that she was the one who could get the impossible loans done when others couldn't. At the time that impressed me.

CAN I VS. SHOULD I

She was asking, "How can I do this?" I doubt very seriously that she ever asked, "Should I do this?"

If I encountered this mentality today, I'd not only reject it; I'd bolt faster than the Roadrunner running from Wile E. Coyote and his Acme Rockets.

In the past, my vetting process for my Bucky 5 was a combination of being around people I was idolized by or those who had gray rules for their lives. My biggest concern was how much money they made, could I learn from them, could we have fun, and could they afford the expensive nature of sharing my lifestyle.

INSTINCTUAL VETTING

My vetting process today starts with someone's presence. If I feel like they're a scumbag, I won't have anything to do with them. I judge fast, and I trust my instincts. If I smell a rat, I'll ask questions very quickly to ascertain whether the person is honest or a phony. I could care less whether someone has made mistakes, gone bankrupt, been divorced, cheated on their dog, etc., etc.

I'm actually more interested in being in friendship and relationship with people who've screwed up and made mistakes, learned and exchanged minds. It shows me a level of consciousness that most perfect performers will never have. Perfect performers actually scare me because they have no emotional understanding of mistakes and the deep scars that are needed for mastery. They also don't have an instinctual skillset for avoiding danger compared to those who've gone through hell like I have.

It would also be kind of hypocritical for me to judge anyone's past considering how many "learning opportunities" I've had with all my swings at bat.

The most important thing for me today when determining who to spend time with is to know that the person I'm with is honest and plays by these three rules:

1. His word is impeccable, the doing matches the saying. When he messes up he owns the mistake and takes total responsibility.
2. She will say what needs to be said.
3. He is focused on adjusting himself by growing, and while grateful for what's in his life, he is looking for ways to make a difference for others on the planet.

Notice, these three things have zero to do with someone's past. The past is only an indication of the present if the inputs are the same and the energy is the same. If the person is doing the same things they did in the past and their past scares me, I won't go near them. If they learned from their past like I did and shifted or are clearly shifting towards truth, I'm very open to the engagement.

I'm very conscious about my Bucky 5, and as much as I love my family and friends from the past, I am very deliberate about how much time I spend with some of them in person or even in thought. Everything has influence, nothing is neutral, and if I know I'm going to be the average of the five people I spend my time with, I'm only going to spend time with those I'm okay with becoming more like.

PROXIMITY

I think one of the mistakes I've made in the past has been friendship by proximity. If someone likes the same restaurant or bar as I do, we're likely to end up in the same place together a lot. But our relationship has little to do with a deeper connection. It's more of a time/space collision accident.

After my reinvention, I'm grateful and totally conscious to my Bucky 5. They're not my nearest neighbors; in fact, only a couple of them even live in the same state as me. My inner team—those I spend a majority of my time with and listen to closest—are people I didn't even know a few years ago. As I shifted into a place of truth, those old friends and acquaintances who were living in the shadows or in quiet desperation without any will to evolve naturally fell away or were repelled by the person I am now. My mind kind of flushed them, to be blunt.

They didn't stick because there was no alignment between who they are today and who I am today.

The only people I spend time with today are those who are in my "tribe." I can say with absolute conviction that my five closest friends are absolutely impeccable with their word. Are yours? I know without a doubt they will do what they say they'll do. Will yours? My Bucky 5 inspire me and push me. When I look at them, I'm pulled towards a higher state of consciousness. What are your Bucky 5 doing for or to you?

I don't remember where I heard this, but I think about it all the time. At the end of my life, I want to know that my life was an example for others to follow, not a warning. Being conscious of your Bucky 5 helps create the tactical alchemy for this to happen.

PROCESS

Discretion of speech is more than eloquence; and to speak agreeably to him with whom we deal is more than to speak in good words or in good order.

—Francis Bacon

Any process of reinvention will certainly require a complete reassessment of the criteria by which you select the people with whom you spend time. The process of finding those individuals who mirror, support, and augment your defined and chosen values begins with your acceptance and/or aspiration to have similar traits and principles.

In other words, in the initial phase of defining your inner circle, your selection criteria will be limited to finding people who are "like you." As the process evolves (and your value and goal definitions become clearer), the selection criteria will evolve into finding people whose company is desired more for their individual vision(s) than its similarity to yours.

It is equally important to be cognizant of the fact that the majority of the people with whom you have voluntary or mandatory contact do not need to adhere to or be judged by the requirements of your inner circle. It is unfair to all parties involved, a waste of time, lacking kindness. Becoming aware of appropriate times and places for releasing your thoughts is the ultimate tool in the art of discretion.

"There is nothing in a caterpillar that tells you it's going to be a butterfly."

—Buckminster Fuller

CHRISTOFER'S STORY

I have always been content with my own company and, for many years, operated under the belief that this incarnation would be one of solitude and contemplation. As a musician I was one hundred percent focused on creating both technical and artistic excellence and did not have much time for people unless I was working on a recording project or performance with them. My few meaningful personal connections were usually with much older individuals with whom the interactions were based much more on a mentor/student relationships than friendship. This suited me well as I have never had any tolerance or skill in the making of small talk and generally found most people's conversational repertoires to be based on urban legend, ignorance and hearsay. If I wanted to learn something new or develop a greater knowledge about something, I would take a course. If I wanted to friend, I had my dog.

This rather callous *raison d'etre* was quite useful in my corporate finance profession as such a clinical detachment allowed me to become highly skilled and highly sought after in both due diligence and contract negotiations. On the due diligence front, I was the person who was called in to find problems and issues that would eventually drive down the price of the target acquisition. If something didn't seem right (misstatement of earnings, a well-disguised related party transaction, etc.), I would lead a crusade to uncover the issue. On the contract side, I was the person who would clinically dissect and argue any potentially negotiable valuation issues with a goal of having the acquirer's representatives (usually lawyers, consultants or accountants) acquiesce to the logic of my findings. When my due diligence work required that I spend considerable time (sometime months) in the target company, I followed a self-imposed rule to have limited interaction (other than tacit pleasantries) with any members of management lest my judgment and emotions be affected by said discourse. I stayed very disconnected socially.

As I progressed through the corporate ranks and started to spend less time on financial/operational analysis and more time on capital markets (arranging debt and equity financing), research on the character, background and experience of the company's management and owners became an important part of my work.

In addition to arranging financing and structuring investments, I was spending a considerable amount of time meeting and speaking with company owners and entrepreneurs, running background checks, and generally digging deep into the chosen individuals' lives. I noticed that the majority of those with whom I was working were generally consistent in their professional lives, though in their personal lives there were huge inconsistencies.

A brilliant and visionary entrepreneur who was devoutly religious and a family man had a cocaine and gambling problem. A brilliant finance manager with an impeccable business and academic pedigree had a secret life of sexual deviance. I started to wonder if the majority of people were just living a secret life and if my investigative way of looking at people had permanently damaged my ability to accept people for who they are.

I hadn't heard of "The Bucky Five," and if someone had asked me about the it, I would have assumed it was some splinter faction of the IRA who were somehow linked to bombing subways. To get on with the story, I decided to make a concerted effort to seek the company of people who were not part of an extended due diligence project. Riding the train back to my home in Kenilworth, I wrote down a list of the attributes that were important to me and would be a requirement for any friendships.

My list was rather simple and contained the required attributes of intelligence, culture (appreciation and interest in art), integrity, financially successful, and good hygiene. Since I was already out on a potential New Age limb, I spent a few moments envisioning the conversations we (my undiscovered friends and I) would have when we met.

A SUDDEN CHANGE OF PERCEPTION

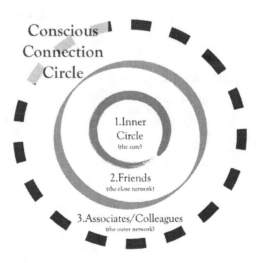

Conscious
Connection
Circle

1.Inner
Circle
(the core)

2.Friends
(the close network)

3.Associates/Colleagues
(the outer network)

There are only two ways to live your life. One is as though nothing is a miracle. The other is as though everything is a miracle."

—Albert Einstein

I forgot about my list of attributes and continued on with my work and life. Around this time I was asked to go to Romania on a telecom project. After landing in Bucharest I took a walk around Revolution Square, looking at the diverse group of street performers which included a female contortionist, a dancing bear and a very talented cellist who was performing the Prelude from Bach's Third Cello Suite. She was an extremely gifted performer and those of us who comprised her audience applauded enthusiastically and filled her case with whatever coins we had. During this little concert there was a fellow standing next to me who also appeared to be enjoying the performance. All of a sudden the dancing bear appeared to attack the contortionist, and the curious crowd quickly dispersed leaving only me and the other gentleman to listen to the final movement of the suite. When the music stopped, we exchanged pleasantries and soon departed for our respective destinations.

The following morning, I gathered my papers and walked the short distance to the bank where we where we were to have the first meeting. Walking into the conference room, I was surprised to see that the lead investor in the project was none other than the person who was standing next to me at the cello recital. To make a long story short, we became great friends and worked on a number of projects together. As we became friends, I was pleasantly surprised to find out that he and his family embodied many of the attributes I had included on my aforementioned list.

It would be a short jump as compared to a giant leap of conjecture to conclude that the composition of the attribute list had something to do with the discovery of a new friendship.

I am, however, certain that my taking time to define a wish list of attributes created a tactical framework for the inclusion of new friends and mitigated a rather harsh and generalized judgment of people. I sometimes wonder how it would have turned out if the dancing bear went after the cellist instead of the contortionist.

SUMMARY

The true mystery of the world is the visible, not the invisible.

—Oscar Wilde

The profound lesson I learned in this first attempt to define my inner circle is that the attributes that I seek in those of my inner circle are ever-present in my life and become manifest when the time is taken to define them. If you do nothing, nothing will happen. If you decide to take the time to define the vision and attributes of your inner circle, you could discover that those persons who embody said attributes are probably not far away from where you stand today. Think about that!

MY CURRENT INNER CIRCLE LIST

1. Integrity/Honesty

   • Do what you say you will do with consistency.
   • Be open about your past, even if it is ugly. If you try to cover things up, it will come out.

2. Intelligence

   - No brain donors. You must a thinker.
   - Absolutely no gossip or urban legend. Think before you speak.

3. Creativity

   - What have you created and what are you excited about creating?
   - What are you creating now?

4. Learning/Improving

   - What are you studying and what are you specifically trying to improve?
   - What can you teach me? What can I teach you?

5. Literate

   - What are you reading now and how much do you read?
   - Are *Vanity Fair* and *People* magazine your idea of a good novel?
   - What kind of music do you listen to and why? Teach me something new.

6. Financially Successful

   - How do you feel about prosperity, and are you prosperous?

- How do you feel about money, and how do you spend what you have (or don't have)?
- How do you feel about money?

7. Amusing & Fun

- Being funny and entertaining (when appropriate) is important. What is humorous in your life?
- What makes you really laugh?

8. Elegant

- Is your use of the language refined or crude?
- Are you discreet with your conversations and information?
- Do you practice gratitude?
- Do you have good hygiene?

QUESTIONS & ACTIONS

1. Is there is someone in your life whose actions, thoughts and influence are dragging you down? Who are they? Why are you spending time with them? Why have you not cut them loose?
2. Of the five people closest to you, which are losers and which are keepers? Change your phone number, move, pretend you don't know them when they call. Can you do this?
3. Write down your Bucky 5 and their state of wealth, health, love, integrity and mission.

11
SIMPLICITY

def.

1. The quality or state of being simple, unmixed, or uncompounded; as the simplicity of metals or of earths.
2. The quality or state of being not complex, or of consisting of few parts; as the simplicity of a machine.
3. Artlessness of mind; freedom from cunning or duplicity; lack of acuteness and sagacity.
4. Freedom from artificial ornament, pretentious style, or luxury; plainness; as simplicity of dress or of language, simplicity of diet, simplicity of life.

On Acquiring More of Everything...

We've got to cut the extraneous out of our lives, and we've got to learn to stem the inflow. We need to think before we buy. Ask ourselves, 'Is that really going to make me happier? Truly?'

—Graham Hill

CHRISTOFER'S STORY

In my adult life, I have moved twelve times. All of my moves have been for purposes of education or employment and, with few exceptions, involved transporting large amounts of stuff that I thought to be valuable. The first of these moves (going to university) was accomplished by loading everything I owned into a Toyota Tercel. The last one required two forty-foot and one twenty-foot shipping containers which were completely full.

I happened to open one of the forty-foot containers last month (which has been sitting in a warehouse for five years) and discovered that absolutely none of the stuff was of any value or interest to me. The problem is that if I want to get rid of the contents of the container, it will require a considerable amount of time and energy. The contents of the containers once interested me enough to spend the time and money purchasing them (and packing them and moving them), and with them came a certain pride of acquisition and ownership. Now the pleasure is gone, and all that remains is the expense of storage and insurance.

SHELTER FROM THE STORM OF ACQUISITION

I live part of the year on a small island in the Grenadines where the only things you can purchase are food, gasoline and basic home/marine hardware. The essential items (food and shelter) are cheap; everything else is expensive. Most business establishments will not accept payment with a credit card or check so the majority of transactions are cash. Being there is an exercise in "not consuming," as there is very little one can purchase. It is possible to go days and sometimes weeks without acquiring anything other than food. The inflow of non-essential items into my home is minimal, and the peace of not being tempted to acquire and collect produces a profound change in the daily rhythm of life.

In contrast, my life in the U.S. is constantly under attack with an unremitting barrage of advertisers' attempts to push their products on me through every possible medium. It is so easy to pull out the credit card and load the car with more stuff, which will invariably end up in the trash or moved to another owner.

DAMION'S STORY

Tokens of success provide a validation that we've made it, a projection of something we're not certain of inside. In my simplifying process, I kind of went from the penthouse to the basement and found the foundation of the ground below me. My experience living in the big house with the flashy car and the AMEX Black card was the never-ending, relentless pursuit of spending and consumption.

I remember when my old mentor Dan (the guy I paid $10,000 a month to for a couple calls and emails) encouraged me to buy the Ferrari and spend a week with him at his castle with my partners. I find it funny that I was paying Dan $10K a month to advise me to buy a quarter-million dollar car and strong arm the bank into loaning me most of the purchase price. I find it ironic that he was supposed to be looking out for me and in retrospect was focusing on his own cash infusion—such as the $70,000 my partners and I shelled out for a week at the castle.

This type of relationship was expensive and elaborate, just the way my old mind needed it to be to satisfy my need for significance. When I found inner peace and significance inside, I no longer had the need to buy my way into it with shiny tokens.

The home I live in is no longer proof or not-proof that I've arrived. I actually feel more satisfied and less stressed the less stuff I have and the less consuming I do.

Over the last couple years in the reinvention process, I've moved a few times and let go of more and more stuff, just like Christofer. Each move into a smaller space has helped me let go of the excess, the things I didn't love. The truth is that most things I don't love and cherish have no reason to be here other than they attempt to quell a **fear of isolation and poverty**.

The biggest problem with the complexity of having more stuff as opposed to the grace and peace of living in simplicity is that it requires our world to be structured in such a way that consumerism must continuously expand and grow or the economy shrinks and recession happens. Thus, encouragement of consumption happens at every turn all around us.

QUESTIONS & ACTIONS

1. If your home was on fire, what are the three things that you would grab on your way out the door?
2. If you had to move tomorrow and you could only take your computer and one suitcase of personal items, what would you put in the suitcase?
3. For a period of one month, try removing (trashing, donating, gifting) one item per day from your home and limiting (with the exception of food) the inflow of non-essential items to one per week.
4. For a period of one week, pay for everything with cash. Put your credit cards and checkbook away.
5. Ask yourself what you love so much that you would keep if you had to move into a space half as big as you currently live in.
6. Walk around your house and ask these questions of everything you encounter: Do I love it? Do I need it? If it's time to let it go, am I going to sell, lend or give it away—and when?

7. Of your total wardrobe, what percent of it do you wear on a regular basis and what percent have you not worn in more than a year? Go into your wardrobe and pick your favorite ten tops and favorite ten bottoms. What's left? And why do you still have it?

EPILOGUE

Our revels now are ended. These our actors,
As I foretold you, were all spirits and are melted
into air, into thin air:
And, like the baseless fabric of this vision,
The cloud-capp'd towers, the gorgeous palaces,
The solemn temples, the great globe itself,
Yea, all which it inherit, shall dissolve
And, like this insubstantial pageant faded,
Leave not a rack behind. We are such stuff
As dreams are made on, and our little life
Is rounded with a sleep.
—William Shakespeare

This book sprang into being almost spontaneously of its own energy. The amazing journey into connection and friendship through the creating of the book has been truly breathtaking and one of the great experiences of both our lives. It was born as a result of our deep desire to teach, to share the evolving story of our lives' journeys, and to gain greater clarity of our own reinventions.

We are honored and humbled by your willingness to spend your time learning with us and look forward to meeting you one day. Please reach out to us and tell us about your reinvention, whether you've just had a trigger event or are well into and deep inside the process. We'd love to hear your story and equally look forward to supporting you in your pursuit of excellence, in creating a spectacular and reinvented life.

The fact is, you have a story of change in your life that was either planned, a product of having no plan, or the outcome of a rogue random occurrence. Regardless of whether you planned it or are simply deciding how to interpret the change, the power is in your hands—or more rightly put, it's entirely in your mind to do with it exactly as you'd like.

We know from our experience of reinventing our lives, going through brutal times and painful transformations, that in the end it's all about your desire, vision and conviction towards your vision. The burning desire to reinvent your life will determine your fate.

In parting, let us share a couple of final thoughts. Death isn't what happens at the end; it's the evidence of change. Without the death of your former self there is no transformation into your true self. Celebrate death and learn to keep dying to find the essence of life. As Frederick Nietzsche once said, "When a snake can't shed it's skin, it cannot survive and must perish."

Be the snake. Let the old you become dust and move into your new skin to explore the rest of your life reinvented.

Blessings, thank you, Namaste.

Damion Lupo & Christofer Ashby

BOOKS AND RESOURCES FROM
CHRISTOFER AND DAMION:

Websites
www.mylifebook.com
www.Yokido.org
www.ashbywindwardfoundation.org

Books
A Course in Miracles—
It's called Work for a Reason—Larry Winget
Your Greatest Power—J. Martin Kohe
The User's Guide to the Human Mind—Shawn T. Smith, PsyD
A Whole New Mind—Dan Pink
Thinking for a Change—John Maxwell
A Little Book on The Human Shadow—Robert Bly
The Ultimate Blueprint for an Insanely Successful Business—
    Keith Cunningham
The Narrow Road—Felix Dennis
The Four Agreements—Miguel Angel Ruiz
The Elephant in The Dark—Christianity, Islam and the Sufis—
    Idries Shah
The Art of the Comeback—Donald Trump
Perfect Health—Deepak Chopra
Be Here Now—Ram Dass
The Way of the Superior Man—David Deida
Or I'll Dress You In Mourning—Larry Collins & Dominique
    Lapierre

Music
Mass for Three Voices—William Byrd
Ode To St. Cecilia—Henry Purcell
Stabat Mater—Giovanni Pergolesi
Lecons Tenebres—Marc-Antoine Charpentier
1 Giant Leap—Jamie Catto and Duncan Bridgeman
Concha Buika—En Mi Piel
Manuel Moreno Junquera (Moraito Chico)—Morao, Morao
Abida Parveen—Kabir by Abida

Programs/Workshops
Lifebook—Lifebook Chicago
4 Day MBA—Keith Cunningham
Journey Into Healing—Chopra Center
The Hoffman Process
The Reinvention Cycle

THE AUTHORS:

DAMION S. LUPO

Raised in Alaska, Damion is part Alaskan, part Texan and 100% Reinvention. He's a four-time college drop out (the final enrollment lasted a mere 45 minutes at the University of Texas). He earned his stripes and cut his teeth in the rough and dirty trenches of real life, becoming a self-made multi millionaire at age 25.

He's the founder of Yokido, a blend of Aikido and Yoga, holds a black belt in Aikido, is a practitioner of yoga and a student of Reiki. He's a lifelong student of Austrian economics and runs a precious metals company based in Austin, Texas.

Damion also enjoys SCUBA diving and traveling the world. He considers himself an artist, author and visionary in human potential through conscious engagement.

Currently he spends his time teaching and lecturing on the art of reinvention. His mantra is to teach by example, to teach via what he does not just by what he says.

Audiences around the world learn from his unique and often painful experiences, allowing him to inspire them to elevate their thinking and achieve a life of fulfillment.

CHRISTOFER C. ASHBY, PHD, MBA

Christofer graduated from California State University at Fullerton with an undergraduate degree in Music. He has multiple graduate degrees including Masters and Doctoral degrees from The University of Southern California, where he attended under full scholarship, and a Masters in Business Administration from The University of Warwick in the United Kingdom. He completed post-doctoral research as a Fulbright Scholar in Seville, Spain.

As a businessman and entrepreneur, he has over 20 years of experience in structured finance, mergers & acquisitions and business development in the telecommunication, banking and insurance sectors. He has been a keynote speaker at The Economist Intelligent Unit, European Venture Capital Association and The Central European Bankers Forum.

As a classical guitarist, he studied in master classes of Andres Segovia, Oscar Ghiglia and Jose Tomas and made six records under the New World and China Record Company Labels. As a Flamenco guitarist, he worked as an accompanist in the studio of Jimenez Enrique Mendoza "El Cojo," and attended masterclasses with Diego Gastor in Moron de la Frontera.

As a philanthropist, Christofer is Chairman of the Ashby Windward Foundation, a private foundation which was founded to improve the lives of the citizens of Grenada, Carriacou and Petite Martinique by providing grants and assistance in the areas of healthcare, medical equipment and education. It has funded over 90 surgical procedures and continues to expand its charitable giving by further assisting in the areas of social welfare and public infrastructure projects.

Dr. Ashby's special interests include aviation where he holds multiple fixed wing and rotorcraft ratings, languages, yoga, and boating. When not travelling, he lives on the island of Carriacou in the Grenadines.

To contact Damion Lupo or Christofer Ashby or for additional information on the Reinvented Life Programs please visit:

Reinvented Life | R

www.ReinventedLife.com

Made in the USA
Charleston, SC
12 December 2012